Intelligence

Intelligence
an introduction

David W. Pyle
School of Teacher Education
Hull College of Higher Education

Routledge & Kegan Paul
London, Boston and Henley

First published in 1979
by Routledge & Kegan Paul PLC
14 Leicester Square, London WC2H 7PH, England
9 Park Street, Boston, Mass. 02108, USA
464 St Kilda Road, Melbourne,
Victoria 3004, Australia and
Broadway House, Newtown Road
Henley-on-Thames, Oxon RG9 1EN, England
Set in Linocomp Plantin by Oxprint, Oxford
and printed in Great Britain by
T.J. Press (Padstow) Ltd, Padstow, Cornwall
© David W. Pyle 1979
No part of this book may be reproduced in
any form without permission from the
publisher, except for the quotation of brief
passages in criticism

Reprinted in 1981 and 1984

British Library Cataloguing in Publication Data

Pyle, David W.
Intelligence
1. Intellect.   2. Cognition in children
I. Title
155.4'13   BF431   79-40786

ISBN 0 7100 0306 4
ISBN 0 7100 0307 2 Pbk

To Eve and Bill

Contents

Preface ix

1 What is intelligence? 1
   A word with many meanings 1
   Problems and objections 4
   Some models of intelligence 6
   A set of highly developed skills 16
   Conclusion and implications 18

2 Can intelligence be measured? 20
   Early historical background 21
   Modern conventional tests (norm-referenced measures) 24
   Criticisms of conventional tests 33
   Innovations in mental measurement (criterion-referenced and diagnostic measures) 36
   Conclusions 47

3 What affects intelligence? 48
   Some important issues 48
   Factors on the inside 50
   Factors on the outside 55
   Attempts to raise IQ 61
   Complex and continuous interactions 64
   Conclusion and implications 66

4 The development of intelligence 68
   The units of intellectual development 70
   Developmental approaches 72
   What pushes thinking forward? 79
   The processes of thinking—another approach 80
   Language in cognitive development—some implications 83

viii *Contents*

    Conclusions 86

5 Intelligence and learning 87
    Could do better? 87
    IQ and school achievement 89
    Intellectual abilities and learning 92
    Events in learning 94
    Mastery learning 98
    Optimal learning environments 99

Further Reading 105

Bibliography 109

Index 121

Preface

This book is for all those who are educationally concerned with the developing abilities of children. It is written as a primer—an introduction to some of the many issues and controversies which riddle the topic of intelligence. I have not written a definitive review of everything ever uttered on the subject, nor have I tried an academic reformulation of issues leading to new, insightful approaches. Rather I have written for people who find more advanced texts difficult to read and understand, either because they lack an overall view of the subject, or because they get weighed down with empirical detail and tend to lose sight of the forest for the trees. I try to provide a conceptual 'map'— that is a sketch of some of the major issues involved, indicating why they are important and what they have to do with the education and teaching of children, and showing how they relate to other important areas. I also suggest which books develop the points discussed, so hopefully directing the reader to more advanced writings with some sense of initial understanding and meaningfulness.

Whilst reiterating the aim of introducing the reader to fairly tough and exacting subject matter, I have also tried to gather some topics and studies together that are not readily available between two covers. There is a tendency in psychology towards books which look at isolated aspects of behaviour. We may read (or attempt to read) a book on memory, another on learning and its difficulties, yet another on personality and emotional problems. We might slip into believing that these areas are separate. Clearly, to a greater or lesser extent, each is related to each other. The divisions are arbitrary devices to help us cope with lots of data and ideas. They might be useful in this respect, or they might blind us to more productive possibilities. Such is the case with books on intelligence. Often the intelligence test and the resulting 'IQ' are the subjects of debate occupying many hundreds of pages, with little reference to other factors. I have tried in this little book to move away from this approach. Whilst I have not been able to examine links with personality and social interaction, for example, I have attempted to move into traditionally separate areas and look at intelligence from a developmental point of view and from a more experimental learning approach. Therefore intelligence, learning and development are subjects of this introduction, and my intention is mainly to escape in part from over-narrow 'IQ' concerns and move towards more educationally profitable topics. More advanced texts (for example, see Resnick (1976) in *Further Reading*) are tending to adopt this eclectic approach, partly in order to study the topic more fruitfully.

Despite occasional attempts to dispense with the notion of 'intelligence', most psychologists and educationalists recognise and utilise an ability dimension in catering for the ways in which individuals differ. The topic of individual differences, however, is by no means a simple one, and this book introduces the reader to some long-standing and current debates. Intelligence may be an hypothetical construct, but it is also one which is practical and which is used by many people in everyday life— in educational and vocational selection, for example. It is, therefore, an extremely important concept to examine, and one which is likely to be around for some considerable time to come. Therefore, because of this theoretical and practical importance, this book takes a theoretical and practical orientation.

Theory invariably informs practice (even if intuitively so) and practitioners are often at pains to evaluate theory against the background of their professional experience. This book is written within this context, and as such simple 'tips' do not appear because they are inappropriate. Each chapter contains implications, either implicit or explicitly stated, for both theory and for practice. The overall aim is not to search for panaceas which might 'improve IQ', but to examine conditions of development and learning and use our present levels of knowledge and understanding to improve educational environments. This is not a static business, however, but one which is evolving and changing as research evidence accumulates. In this sense, an educationally useful approach is discussed which views intelligence as a set of highly developed skills (but not in a narrow behavioural sense) and processes. The learning environment should be able to be designed which will provide opportunity for any child to develop and utilise these skills and processes as far as possible. Within this educational context, the issue of heredity and environment is discussed. Currently efforts are being made to view educational assessment in a more open-ended way—that is to see assessment as part of a dynamic process relating to learning and the curriculum in an integrated fashion. In this book, these themes are discussed with regard to intelligence within the context of learning and development.

I should like to thank the following people for reading earlier drafts of the book, and providing valuable and encouraging comments: Jackie Collinson (Headteacher), David Bowen (Principal Lecturer in Education) and Peter Randall (Senior Educational Psychologist). What is left, of course, is entirely my own responsibility!

Chapter 1

What is intelligence?

The short answer to the question 'What is intelligence?' is that we are just not sure! If we close our eyes to this very important question, important both theoretically and practically, it will not, of course, cease to become important or disappear. We shall start to discuss this question in this chapter and continue this discussion through the entire book. We shall not be able to provide an answer—this would be an impossible task. However, it is hoped to squash some persistent myths and to offer some practical advice about some very relevant issues for educationalists, including teachers, headteachers and administrators.

So this chapter starts by taking a look at the various meanings given to the term 'intelligence', then briefly examines some 'models' which researchers have devised—various views of the form and structure of intelligence—and after discussing a modern approach to the topic, some initial implications will be listed which will be followed up in later chapters.

A word with many meanings

One of the first things to realise is that the word 'intelligence' is a 'situation-specific' word. That is, the word is used in various situations (rightly or wrongly) and thus takes on various meanings depending upon the particular situation. There are many words or terms in our language which are situation-specific, and psychology certainly takes its fair share! When we speak of learning, or motivation, or personality and so on, we are more than likely using each word in a specific way depending on a specific situation.

When using the word intelligence, then, we may be referring to a number of situations, and the following instances are probably the most important to keep clearly distinguished in our minds. These various meanings, and they are not the only ones by any means, are very much the starting points for what follows in the rest of this book.

(a) Intelligence might be taken to mean 'ability'—what a person *can* do at this moment (Dockrell, 1970). This might be decided upon by just looking at how a person behaves in certain situations, e.g. changing a car tyre or writing an essay, or by assessing him more objectively by some test of ability. Intelligence here is taken to mean present levels of performance.

(b) But intelligence might be used as being synonymous with a different kind of 'ability'—what a person is thought *capable* of doing in the future on the strength of information gathered in the present. Here a person is assessed, again either subjectively by looking at his behaviour, or objectively by some ability test, and on this information judgments are made about his potential levels of performance (rightly or wrongly). Intelligence here may be taken to mean capacity or the ability to learn in the future, and because this cannot be observed it is often given names such as 'hypothetical construct', 'latent trait' and the like.

(c) There are many issues here in (a) and (b), but one important aspect to bring into the light now is to distinguish clearly, when necessary and appropriate to do so, as to whether we are talking about some private, and possibly biased and prejudiced, subjective decision about the 'intelligence' of a person, or whether we are talking about measured intelligence—a person's results on some test of ability, generally referred to as the IQ (Intelligence Quotient). Indeed, intelligence has been seen as something which can be measured—that is as a product. It is but a short step from this to reckon that we all *possess* intelligence to a greater or lesser degree. This is taken further in chapter 2.

(d) Intelligence might be taken to mean the speed at which a child is developing mentally—'He is a bright lad for his age.' The processes of intellectual (or cognitive) development are ones which enable a child to understand and know what the world is all about, and at various stages of growing up these processes undergo quite revolutionary changes. So here we have a further refinement of intelligence—it may be taken to have different meanings at various stages of development. This is dealt with in more detail in chapter 4.

(e) Intelligence may refer to the ability to profit from experience. For example, one might read of animals and insects displaying stereotyped behaviour (the bee is not able to alter its dance routines!) but a human being is more flexible and versatile, is able to remain plastic and respond to situations not in fixed ways, but in different and appropriate ways. So, a person might be labelled intelligent if he is 'effective' or 'adequate' or 'capable' in some general way. This leads us into the next usage.

(f) Intelligence has been given many actual 'definitions' by various thinkers and researchers. If we listed all of these we would fill this book and still not know what the word meant! Let us look at just a few examples. Notice how each definition emphasises particular abilities and skills which are thought to be important, and how most say something about the ability to reason:

Binet: to judge well, to comprehend well, to reason well.

Spearman: general intelligence which involves mainly the 'education of relations and correlates'.

Terman: the capacity to form concepts and to grasp their significance.

Vernon: stresses a simple and non-specific definition, such as 'all-round thinking capacity' or 'mental efficiency'.

Burt: innate, general, cognitive ability.

Heim: intelligent activity consists in grasping the essentials in a situation and responding appropriately to them.

Wechsler: the aggregate or global capacity of the individual to act purposefully, to think rationally and to deal effectively with the environment.

Piaget: adaptation to the physical and social environment.

Basically, one finds that the biologist would stress the ability to adapt to the demands of the environment; the educationalist the ability to learn; some psychologists emphasise the measurement of the ability to reason and other cognitive functions, others the development of those functions; and probably the layman would mumble something about 'common sense'! One suggestion has been made by a number of workers to try to get around the definition problem, and this has been termed the 'operational' or 'working' definition: intelligence is what intelligence tests measure. This type of definition has served the physical sciences well during their early development, and might therefore be useful to us in certain situations. Vernon (1960) and Guilford (1967) discuss the biological, experimental, psychological, developmental and operational approaches to the study of intelligence.

Some writers would argue that intelligence is not the same as other psychological terms like 'learning', 'thinking', 'problem-solving', 'attainment' or 'achievement' (for example, Turner, 1977). Others would argue that these terms are not qualitatively different and to a great extent over-lap (for example, Humphreys, 1971; McFarland, 1971). This important practical as well as theoretical problem is discussed in chapters 4 and 5, and we shall argue there that intelligence is not qualitatively different from learning, thinking and development.

Obviously we are up against some formidable problems, and it might ease the reader into the main issues if we looked briefly at some problems and objections.

Problems and objections

One basic problem has already been mentioned. Basically, what intelligence is taken to mean depends all too often on the point of view of the researcher or the writer. Thus, any orientation or perspective adopted leads to a possible different catch-phrase, and this is clearly messy and not too respectable in the world of science. Another objection here is that looking at individual 'qualities' is misleading—e.g. how does a person's reasoning and flexibility aid his learning? And further, should we not include personality and motivational factors in any definition—e.g. persistence and drive? So, intelligence is too often viewed in a narrow, one-sided fashion. Some would prefer to see the topic left quite open and 'polymorphous'. Miles (1957) discusses the idea of polymorphous concepts and analyses a whole range of problems associated with definitions. He maps out six ways of using the word 'definition' and critically analyses Burt's and Wechsler's definitions of intelligence in this context. Not everyone is over-concerned with such criticisms. McNemar (1964), for example, is quite uninterested in this sort of philosophical analysis of intelligence and virtually dismisses Miles's (1957) discussion on definitions. Rather he says we should concentrate on the business of measuring 'response products to standardized situations', and he noted that 'studies of individual differences never come to grips with the process, or operation, by which a given organism achieves an intellectual response' (McNemar, 1964).

Another very important problem is the actual grammatical use of the word intelligence. This point is not quite so academic as it might appear at first sight. 'Intelligence' is often used as a noun and as such is awarded some status—it makes us think that the word is referring to something quite real and tangible and concrete (a quantity of something in the brain, perhaps). This is very wrong. If we use the word as an adjective, then we speak in terms of intelligent behaviour, and intelligence is rather a matter of ways of behaving and acting, and not something that a person has. Technically, this objection is known as reification—one reifies a concept if that concept is awarded a status that it cannot have.

Ryle (1949) severely criticised what he, as a philosopher, took to be conceptual mistakes made by psychologists in their writings on the nature of intelligence. He thought it wrong to suppose that there is some kind of force which lies behind, or explains behaviour. Spearman, for example, is therefore under attack for adopting the notion of 'mental energy'.

Now this is not just some dry, didactic point! If the term 'intelligence' ought to read 'intelligent behaviour', then we are saying that it can only be known by its effects (or its properties)—what actually makes up intelligent behaviour. And this cannot be used to explain other areas of behaviour—it cannot become explanatory. Thus, if a child is a 'good learner' or 'poor learner', it does not make much sense in explaining this in terms of intelligence—he is a good learner because he is intelligent. We still are left with the task of explaining the intelligent behaviour. An analogy may help. Take the words energy (noun) and energetic (adjective) and a person's skill at gardening. If we said that he was a poor gardener because he was not very energetic (or a poor learner because he was not very intelligent), then we are still left with the task of explaining the concept of energy (or intelligence). This is a central point and is developed further in the book. (See also Guilford 1967; Bijou, 1976).

Another stumbling-block is that some definitions can be regarded as simply incorrect, depending upon your point of view. This point has a wide and important connotation. Take, for instance, those definitions that stress in-born, innate, native ability (e.g. Burt). The implication made here is that one is *born* with abilities. This is clearly quite incorrect. To be more precise one has to say that a person inherits the *potentiality* for developing some ability rather than inherits that ability as such. This issue is dealt with in chapter 3, so we will not pursue the matter further here. However, it does lead us on to another major objection.

Vernon (1969) and others (see for example, Berry and Dasen, 1974) would argue strongly that any definition of intelligence must take into account the culture in which an individual is reared. That is, intelligence is inextricably interwoven with the beliefs, values, language, concepts and orientations of a particular group or race of people. We often refer to a range of skills valued by one community at a particular time and virtually assume that the whole world holds similar values. But Cole and Bruner (1971) for instance warn us that this is often not the case, and clearly state the problems in inferring certain psychological processes from apparent cultural differences. It makes no sense to speak of intelligence in isolated ways, and attempts to divorce intelligence from the culture in which an individual is living are doomed from the start. This point is examined further in chapter 3.

So there are many problems and objections. What might be fairly correctly stated before moving on? We are probably on safer ground at this stage by regarding intelligence less as an entity and more as a process, or set of processes—less of a 'thing' and more of an 'abstraction'. A comparison with the word 'digestion' here might be quite useful: it is not an entity which can be touched and directly observed, but a set of processes in the body. We also need to have some kind of framework or overall picture with which to work. Such a 'taxonomy' helps in analysing and mapping out important variables which might help explain a wide range of research findings. These variables, as Vernon (1971) points out, are often referred to as abilities, factors and dimensions.

To see what these might be, we now move on to look briefly at different models of intelligence and examine their components—not as entities so much, but as abilities and as processes.

Some models of intelligence

Psychometric or test-based models

When a great many tests are given to a considerable number of people, the tester ends up with lots of scores and results. He will analyse these scores in certain ways, and the results of his analyses might provide him with some ideas as to the nature of the abilities he thinks he has been measuring. So before we look at these so-called psychometric

What is intelligence?

models or frames of reference based on tests, we should bear two initial points in mind.

(i) the models are the results of tests:
(ii) the names given to parts of the models are labels attached to the results of statistical analyses of the tests.

These statistical techniques are referred to by their technical names of 'correlation coefficients' and 'factor analysis'. This usually allows many 'variables' to be analysed, called 'multi-variate' analysis.

Two-factor model

One of the earliest workers in this area of intelligence was Charles Spearman. He built upon the earlier work of Francis Galton and Karl Pearson, the inventors of the correlation coefficient. This is a number (not greater than 1.0) which indicates to what degree test results of one kind are associated with results of another kind. Spearman, during the early years of this century, gave various tests of mental ability (memory, reasoning, etc.) to many children (1904). He computed the degree to which each test 'agreed' with each of the other tests, that is, determined all the combinations of correlation. He noticed that the tests were 'positively correlated'—this means that if children scored well on one test, they would tend to score well on others, and so on. So this led Spearman to conclude that all the tests had something in common: some 'factor' was involved in all the tests, and all the tests were measuring this common factor. He named this common factor 'g', which stands for 'general intelligence'. But because all the tests did not produce exactly the same results, each had a smaller, more 'specific' ability associated—and these smaller factors he named 'Ss' or 'specific abilities'. Thus, the earliest model of intelligence was Spearman's two-factor theory, and it is summarised in diagrammatic form in figure 1.1.

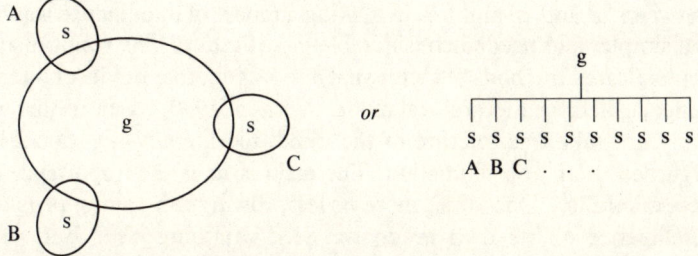

Figure 1.1 Diagrams illustrating Spearman's model of intelligence: general ability + specific abilities (A,B...)

CHARLES SPEARMAN = "General Intelligence" = "g" ⊃ a factor common to all "specific" abilities.

What is intelligence?

According to this model, intelligence is composed mainly of mental energy or general ability which will 'flow' into most if not all of a person's activities: understanding what is read, understanding instructions, filling in complicated forms, planning a day's jobs, reading a bus timetable, etc. The idea was that we all possess 'g' to some level or degree, and the main difference between people's mental ability could be summarised as differences in general intelligence. People will, however, differ in very specific and particular ways because of the smaller specific abilities, so one person will be skilled at car mechanics, another at playing a guitar, and so on (and yet these activities are also under some 'g' control, of course).

In developing his two-factor model, Spearman also developed the technique of 'Factor Analysis'. If a researcher has many tests and he has worked out all the correlations between them, he can apply the techniques of factor analysis which will help him determine whether there is some pattern to be found in the test scores—do some tests cluster closely together, are some tests left quite isolated, seemingly unrelated to other results? The first cluster might be labelled a 'verbal' factor, the second a 'perceptual' factor and so on.

Spearman's original two-factor model came under some considerable criticism, mainly because of further research using the factor analysis technique which he himself had developed! The essential problem was 'g'—i.e. was the process of intelligence as straightforward as this, just one, unitary ability? Was there more to the picture?

Hierarchical model

Work by Cyril Burt (1949) and Philip Vernon during the late forties and fifties established almost beyond doubt that the distinction between 'g' and 's' abilities in making a model of intelligence was far too simple, and needed considerable modification. The result, using sophisticated methods of factor analysis, was another model of intelligence, called the hierarchical model. Vernon (1950) warns us that we must not take this 'picture of the mind' too literally—it should be regarded as an approximation. The main issue is the importance of general ability. Does this, more or less, distinguish among people's intelligence on its own or do we need somthing else? Burt and Vernon's efforts in investigating this question led to the formulation of the model shown in figure 1.2.

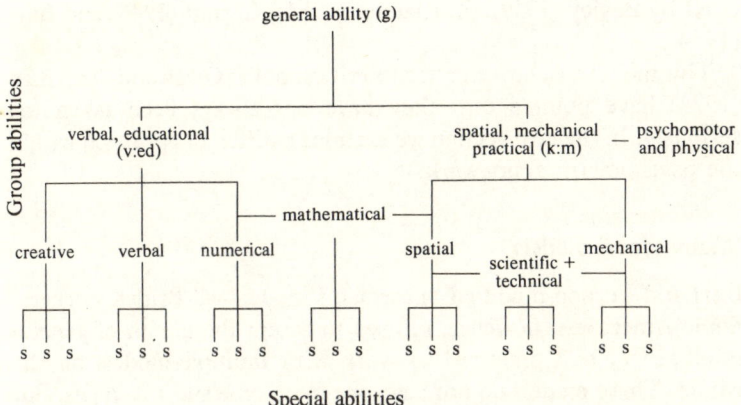

Figure 1.2 Diagram of the hierarchical group-factor theory, showing the main general and group factors underlying tests relevant to educational and vocational achievements.
(Adapted from P. E. Vernon, *Intelligence and Cultural Environment*, London, Methuen, 1969, p. 22. Reproduced with kind permission of Associated Book Publishers Ltd, London.)

This model indicates that there is no simple distinction between general intelligence and particular specific abilities. There is a need to pull them apart and substitute a collection of important *group* abilities in between. Thus, the difference between two people's intelligence can be accounted for not solely in terms of their respective general intelligence, but more in the region of 40 per cent due to 'g'. The remaining difference is due to other abilities (or intelligences), and these are grouped roughly under two headings: verbal and practical (spatial, perceptual, mechanical). According to this model, then, children and adults may differ considerably in how skilled they are in these two main areas (and, of course, in 'g'), although at the same time most people who are good at verbal tests will also tend to score above average on the practical type tests (since 'g' flows into both areas). Then, as we move down the tree, we are able to split the group abilities into smaller component units, being relatively less influential. And right at the bottom are Spearman's specific abilities. We shall return to the implications of this model later on in this chapter, but we can indicate here that this view emphasises an idea that intelligence changes in organisation with age—this is known as differentiation of abilities. This concept is not so different from that used by developmental psychologists like Piaget (1967) and experimental evidence is cited by Bayley (1949), Hofstaetter (1954), Garrett (1946) and Burt (1954).

This model has, however had its critics, but as Owen and Stoneman (1972) have pointed out, they have not always been taken too seriously. In the next section we examine a different approach within the psychometric framework.

'Many types' models

Burt and Vernon modified Spearman's model—all British workers. Some Americans, however, refused to accept the notion of general intelligence, and preferred to work with multiple-models on the whole. These models do not have one main type and sub-types, but just many quite separate abilities. This now brings us to the work of Americans then, and in particular Thurstone and Guilford.

Using tests and factor analytic methods (only of a different type) Thurstone (e.g. 1938 and 1948) found a number of 'Primary Mental Abilities' (often abbreviated as PMAs)—these abilities were held to be all quite basic, with none assuming more importance than any other. The PMAs are shown here—each has a battery of tests for use in schools, designed on the basis of Thurstone's research findings, and are still in use today (see chapter 2).

Thurstone's Primary Mental Abilities

Verbal comprehension: the ability to understand the meaning of words

Word fluency: the ability to think of words rapidly as in rhyming words and anagrams

Number: the ability to work with numbers and compute

Space: the ability to visualise space (e.g. recognise figures in various orientations)

Memory: the ability to recall word-pairs/sentences

Perceptual speed: the ability to grasp visual details quickly

Reasoning: the ability to find general rules on basis of partial information

So it would seem that the British and American models are essentially very different. However, the gap between the positions was more or less resolved over the years. Basically, the problem is due to the varieties of statistical techniques used and the age of subjects. We need not concern ourselves with the details here, and simply say that a 'second-order' factor analysis (apply a second analysis to the results of the first) using children not only adults, showed that 'g' seems to be involved in all the PMAs: thus we are back in essence to the hierarchical model. Thurstone did feel, however, that a broad profile of an individual's mental abilities was more useful than a single, overall measure.

Another American researcher, however, remains adamant that any model of intelligence based on 'g' and broad group factors is still far too simple a view of the human intellect. Guilford (1967) has stipulated that at least 120 unique intellectual abilities exist, and to lump them all together under broad headings (e.g. verbal abilities) does considerable injustice to the richness and depth of the human intellect. Figure 1.3 represents his model of intelligence.

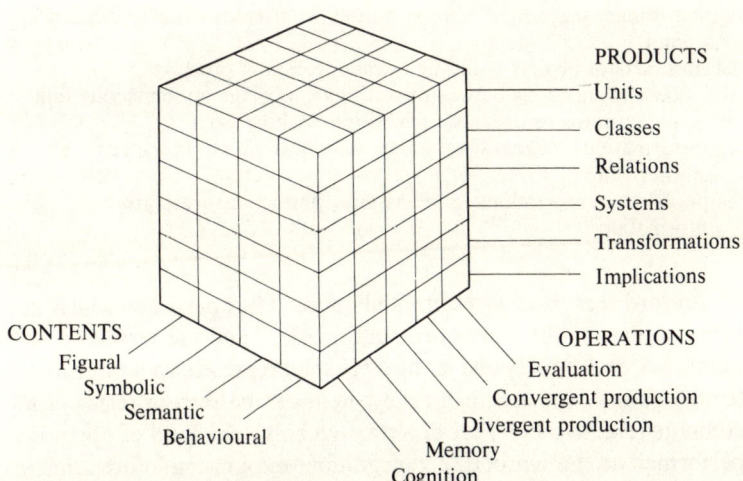

Figure 1.3 The structure of intellect model
(Adapted from J. P. Guilford and R. Hoepfner, *The Analysis of Intelligence, gence,* New York, McGraww Hill, 1971, p. 19. Reproduced with kind permission of McGraw-Hill Book Company, New York.)

Contents

Mental tasks into four categories:
Figural: concrete material of the type perceived directly by senses
Symbolic: concerned with letters, numbers and so on

12 *What is intelligence?*

Semantic: concerned with verbal meanings and ideas
Behavioural: information involved in human interaction (essentially non-verbal)

Operations

Five ways of treating mental information:
Cognition: understanding, knowing and/or discovering
Memory: recalling and recognising
Divergent production: thinking outwards to generate several possible answers/ideas
Convergent production: deducing one correct answer from given information
Evaluation: comparing information with known information and making a judgment concerning criterion satisfaction

Products

Each of the twenty ways of combining contents and operations are manifested under six ways of knowing, understanding or conceiving information:
Units: things, segregated wholes, figures on grounds (usually labelled by a noun)
Classes: sets of objects with one or more common properties
Relations: connections between two things, a bridge or connecting link
Systems: patterns or organisations of interlocking parts
Transformations: changes, revisions, modifications from one state to another state
Implications: expectations, anticipations, predictions from given information

Guilford sees three faces of intelligence. The operations which the brain applies to the contents of information, and the resulting products. So, each small cube in the large solid represents a unique intellectual ability. An intelligence-test item can be seen in terms of its contents (e.g. symbols: set of letter symbols), the kind of operation performed on the symbols (e.g. cognition: recognising information in a symbolic form), and the resulting product (e.g. unit: word answer). With four types of content, five possible operations and six products, Guilford is saying, in effect, that there are at least 120 ways of being intelligent, and his research team are drawing up a test for each one!

Many psychologists have a great deal of respect for Guilford's analysis and his effort to broaden the view of intelligence. His model, for instance, is based upon evidence drawn from genetics, neurology, the biological sciences, areas of experimental psychology like memory, and he incorporates such aspects of behaviour as divergent thinking (often taken to be a crude measure of creative talent). However, the system may not be upheld by the outcome of the research effort, and it may have to be seriously modified. In any case, it may be too bulky for use in any practical educational situation. Unless, that is, we follow Guilford's advice: 'If education has the general objective of developing the intellects of students, it can be suggested that each intellectual factor provides a particular goal at which to aim' (1959). So we may be able to use the model in planning and it could make us think about the nuts and bolts of the thinking process, and how we can design a curriculum to accelerate and enrich these. This is pondered further in chapters 4 and 5.

Other psychometric models

We can mention briefly two other models based on the test-factor analysis approach. These models have been described by Cattell (1971) and Jensen (1970, 1973b).

Cattell actually splits 'g' into two parts: fluid intelligence or g_f – this is a measure of the influence of biological factors and is comparable to inherited ability; as such it is free from influence of the culture (culture fair, or culture free) and education and experience, and is held to flow into a wide variety of intellectual activities. The second one is crystallised intelligence or g_c – this is a measure of the outcome of such cultural and educational experiences. So, Cattell claims to have split 'g' into two parts, and further claims to have found tests to measure both. As we shall presently see (here and in chapter 3) there are some very powerful arguments to counteract such immense claims; we shall simply state here that in practice it is very difficult to be able to split 'g' up: g_f and g_c tend to 'co-operate' and are difficult to separate.

Jensen's ideas about intelligence are related to those of Cattell. Jensen sees mental functioning as falling under two types, or levels, of ability: Level I is called 'associative ability'—it is essentially the capacity to receive stimuli and store and later recall the material, thus being synonymous with memory processes on a fairly mechanical, associative level. Level II is a very different proposition—'cognitive ability' involving the transformation and manipulation of information, and is centrally involved in conceptual and abstract reasoning tasks. There is a one-way relationship between the two levels—Level II depends on efficient functioning of Level I, but not vice versa. These two levels are seen as end points over a continuum. At one end (Level I) little processing of material is required, just a mechanical memorising ability. The other end (Level II) involves considerable manipulation of ideas and material in order to solve conceptual problems. Jensen suggests that aspects of the culture also need to be taken into account for a fuller picture of mental functioning, and so another continuum is introduced, being 'orthogonal' or uncorrelated with Levels I and II. This second continuum, or dimension is related to Cattell's fluid and crystallised forms of 'g'. At one end is 'culture-free' (fluid) material to be learnt, and at the other 'culture-loaded' (crystallised) material. Jensen, therefore, introduces a biological, genetic component into his discussion, and makes much of this, by relating his ideas to the educational scene.

The implications of these ideas are discussed in chapter 3. But the theory is not without its critics. Jarman (1978) holds that many research findings on memory do not fit the Level I-II model at all well, and he discusses an alternative cognitive model, which incorporates Jensen's ideas in an allegedly more efficient manner. This alternative model is very similar to the ones discussed in chapters 2 and 4 (see figures 2.5 and 4.6).

Other approaches

Large criticisms can be made of the test-based approach to the study of intelligence, and they are largely concerned with the over-reliance on tests and statistical techniques in describing a person at a particular point in time and, moreover, in predicting the person's probable status at some future time. The researcher attaches names to what are in effect no more than statistical results, and these are then viewed as 'factors of the mind' with some predictive quality. By definition, this approach is geared to studying groups, and when it comes to applying results to an actual individual, the procedure becomes even more suspect.

Other criticisms are also often made, and these relate very much to the section above on Problems and Objections in the definition of intelligence: e.g. just what are the tests measuring in the first place? More technically, Eysenck (1967) notes that mental *speed* is a critical factor which is not taken into account usually. We return to these points in chapter 2.

Our purpose here is to point out other approaches to forming models of intelligence, though these also are subject to various criticisms from various quarters. An example is the developmental approach of Jean Piaget, which is discussed in chapter 4. We shall just say here that he views intelligence as something quite active and changing—that is, he takes a dynamic approach. Intelligence is seen as an active, ongoing process, where subtle 'conflicts' upset the mental state of equilibrium, with the child finding better and more effective ways of coping with his world. For Piaget, the nature of intelligence is a process of organisation and adaptation which is forever changing—and not an entity or quantity (as the psychometric models do tend to lapse into).

Another approach, which is not far removed from Piaget's is that of D. O. Hebb (1949). His views help to overcome some of the problems we have previously raised. Hebb's thesis is that early experience as a baby and young infant, encourages the formation of 'assemblies' of neurons, or nerve cells. Put very simply, an area of brain tissue (filled with a network of minute 'wires') becomes involved in working together for some activity. These are known as 'schemata', a term also used by Piaget. The more schemata available means that past experience is being built up and integrated into some framework. Any new activity becomes charged with all that has gone before. In this way, an individual builds up an enormous storehouse of concepts and skills, and these are learned. Thus, a child learns to use the perceptual apparatus he may have, he learns to imagine, to reason, and most important he learns how to learn. Now, we must have the necessary 'machinery' for this—a central nervous system, which includes the brain, and other body-systems, and these are developed very much under the control of 'genes' which are inherited from one's parents. Thus, there are two main factors operating here: there is the hereditary factor (genotype) which determines the biological capacity of the body, and there is the factor of experience (phenotype). And Hebb's thesis takes these factors into account in describing intelligence: he stipulates two types of intelligence (1) *Intelligence A* which is the innate potential; the capacity of the central nervous system to deal with schemata; the capacity of development. That is, 'the possession of a good brain and good neural metabolism'. (The genotype.) Intelligence A is not observable and not measurable. (2) *Intelligence B* which is the functioning of the brain and CNS which we observe indirectly in an individual's behaviour and thinking; the result of the 'interaction' between intelligence A and the environment. What an individual does—his observed behaviour. (The phenotype.) Intelligence B can be inferred and sampled via tests. Hebb (1966) has said that Intelligence A and B are not entirely separate. Intelligence A is a necessary component of B—clearly without a brain and a nervous system there would be no functioning of that system. He also stresses that Intelligence B can be lowered by constitutional factors like brain damage at birth, and by environmental factors (see chapter 3).

Can we be more specific as to just what Intelligence B is made of? Ferguson (1954) discusses the skills of thinking which have been distilled from experience in a variety of contexts—this means that they can be transferred from one situation to a variety of other situations. Vernon (1969) makes a similar point about Intelligence B, and holds that it 'is the cumulative total of the schemata or mental plans built up through the individual's interaction with his environment, in so far as his constitutional equipment allows' and these plans include perceptions, practical skills and thinking. We shall certainly return to this important approach to intelligence and especially so in chapter 4, but the main points to bear in mind are that (i) neither intelligence A nor B can be observed directly, and (ii) guessing intelligence B, the present performance, is better than guessing intelligence A, the potential, and (iii) that present mental efficiency (B) is built up in early life through the interactions of the environment.

A set of highly developed skills

Before the main conclusions and implications are drawn together, we will examine the newly emerging view that intelligence can be viewed as a whole range of highly developed and integrated skills. This view, although carefully expounded by modern psychologists (e.g. Howe, 1975), is by no means new, and indeed Binet wrote the following just before his death (1909):

> a child's mind is like a field for which an expert farmer has advised a change in the method of cultivating, with the result that in place of desert land, we now have a harvest. It is in this particular sense . . . that we say that the intelligence of children may be increased. One increases that which constitutes the intelligence . . . namely the capacity to learn, to improve with instruction.

After Binet died in 1911, many of his remarks were ignored and many 'myths' about the nature of general intelligence crept in—one for example, being that it is fixed and constant. But in recent years the whole topic has received a great deal of examination, and many psychologists are returning to the writings of Binet (for example Hunt, 1961).

From Vernon's hierarchical model, Guilford's structure of intellect model, and Piaget's and Hebb's approaches, it is quite clear that the processes of learning and developing are closely interwoven, and both are closely related to intelligence in an individual. What this implies, within biological limits, is that a child learns to be intelligent, in that he acquires a great many skills in his interactions with the environment. Implied here is that intelligence is not only composed of different elements, or abilities, but intelligence is also involved in the way in which the abilities are selected and combined in the solution of problems (Sattler, 1974). Guilford would say that there are 120 or so of these skills; Vernon would probably say that it involved working down from general intelligence through the group factors in the hierarchy, known as 'differentiation' of abilities. Hunt (1971) raises a similar possibility: 'Readiness for any given kind of training or encounter with circumstances is not a matter of fixed intelligence, it is a matter of linguistic and cognitive skills which have been developed in the course of the child's life history'. These views also help in understanding the problem of not using intelligence as an explanatory concept—measured intelligence is a pointer as to how well a child does in certain tests: it does not explain why he does well, or badly. Intelligence cannot be independent of a child's learning history. As Vernon (1969) points out, 'Intelligence then refers to the totality of concepts and skills, the techniques or plans for coping with problems, which have crystallised out of a child's previous experience'. Humphreys (1971) similarly states that there are no qualitative differences between intelligence and achievement. They are, he holds, quantitatively different in breadth—intellectual achievement is broader, encompassing principles of learning and development. Hamilton and Vernon (1976) consider a whole range of evidence that leads them to conclude that cognitive capacities which emerge and reach full competence are the 'essential raw materials of intelligence'. These are perception, the formation and use of concepts, linguistic skills, and the conditions and processes of learning and attention. Thereby, intelligence is perceived more usefully as an 'effect' rather than as a 'cause'.

Some writers have built upon this line of argument. They critically discuss the use of psychometric approaches, with the emphasis often on 'g' and all the associated business of IQ test, classifying of individuals and predicting their future on the strength of such scores, and this often is seen as particularly poor practice for slow learners and mentally handicapped children and adults. Dunn (1968) has called for

18 What is intelligence?

new techniques to measure the ability to learn, and this point has been taken up by Leach and Raybould (1977). They argue that in order to decide how a child will profit from learning opportunities and the most effective ways of enhancing learning, rather than rely on IQ tests and notions of low intelligence, one should design and carry out a 'mini learning experiment' with that child. On a similar note, Clarke and Clarke (1974) reject 'single-shot sampling of an area of behaviour, and from this an estimate of capacity inferred'. They argue that for the severely subnormal, at least, IQ is not suitable. The alternative is to devise and execute a substantial experimental study which will be designed to stimulate otherwise dormant processes of learning and development. Indeed it is often the case that adults are too preoccupied with the ability and intelligence of children, and are too eager to explain poor school performance in terms of low ability—if a child is a poor reader, for instance, they allocate the cause to some hypothetical trait or construct called intelligence. Perhaps we should not be too eager to make such a decision and rather concentrate on the 'task'—in this case stick to reading skill, and investigate this area with a view to future improvement. We should only delegate responsibility to 'underlying processes of intelligence' if we have sound reasons for so doing. We return to this very important issue in chapter 5.

If these views are correct (and a good deal of evidence suggests that they do have some substance—e.g. see evidence cited in chapter 3) then some very fundamental questions arise which will be examined in more detail later in the book. For instance, if a child is learning a range of highly developed skills, then can intelligence levels be fixed? Can measures of intelligence (IQ) be seen as achievement measures (in a similar, yet broader way to reading and number tests)? How active is the child in the development of his own intelligence? Can a child be taught to be intelligent?

⌈ READ ⌉

Conclusion and implications

Some initial implications can now be listed—initial because many of these points will receive further attention in the following pages.

    1 We can confidently list certain points which intelligence may *not* to taken to mean:
    (a) intelligence is not simply some capacity to learn:
    (b) intelligence is not some entity or substance;

(c) intelligence is not unitary in nature (simply 'g', or even worse, 'IQ').

(d) intelligence is not the explanatory concept it is often taken to be.

2 However one defines intelligence, it must be seen as multifaceted: many-sided, not one-sided. This implies that people can be intelligent in many different ways (over and above their general ability) and these ways probably develop with age from childhood to adulthood. It follows, then, that every child is a 'possessor of multiple resources', in fact 'several potential individuals' (Vernon).

3 Intelligence may not be fixed (as such) but flexible, as children learn a whole array of skills. If the onus is on learning, then this has obvious implications for teaching. Perhaps we ought to play down the emphasis on intelligence and rather concentrate upon the teaching and learning of these skills, and often these might be 'task-oriented'—as with reading, for example.

4 Intelligence is not able to be directly measured. Innate intelligence cannot be measured, according to Hebb (at least) and present performance can only be inferred by sampling bits of it through observation and tests—this means, essentially, informed guessing, and stands a chance, therefore, of being incorrect.

5 Any decision about a child's intelligence should not be taken lightly because all the above theoretical considerations (and practical implications) lead us to guard against any simple and easy 'rule of thumb' thinking. Decisions about general ability and hypothetical levels of intelligence often mean that children are allocated positions in some rank-order. Those relegated to the lower divisions on such criteria can be 'damned' forever in educational situations. The evidence we examine in subsequent chapters strongly suggests that this common practice does a grave injustice to the complexities and potentials of such children's minds. Moreover, when one examines closely the 'IQ' test, much is left to be desired, and it is to this topic that we now turn.

Chapter 2

Can intelligence be measured?

This question as it stands is too big, too unmanageable, for any answer to be given. It was stressed in chapter 1 that whatever intelligence is, it is a complex affair and so attempts to measure should be regarded with caution and care. In a sense, any measure will reflect the model (or structure) which one has in mind, and we have seen that this can range from one global concept of 'g' to many more specific skills. But what we must bear in mind is that we are definitely talking of more than a single issue—intelligent behaviour consists of a range of skills, albeit interlocking to a certain degree, and this is what is stressed when writers refer to the multi-faceted nature of intelligence. Any measure should therefore attempt to acknowledge this complex view and in cases where results are presented as only in a single number—the IQ score is obtained from many quick, group tests—they should be treated with considerable caution. This point is very important when making decisions about individuals. One can be a little less cautious when looking at group trends.

So we must start by emphasising the type of intelligence under analysis and measurement. One very severe warning and reminder is that given by Hebb—we cannot measure, in any way, innate intelligence (Intelligence A), the genotype. Thus IQ tests are not measures of innate potential. All we can attempt to refine are our ways of tapping the phenotype (Intelligence B) the results of the interplay of genetic endowment (A) with environmental experiences. We can only guess at B through our measures; we can only refine the samples and infer 'intelligence'.

Therefore, IQ being the result of certain tests, based upon the psychometric approach outlined in chapter 1, is not entirely synonymous with the complex notions of intelligence—it is an informed guess resulting from the sampling of selected thinking skills. Although writers often slip into using 'IQ' to refer to 'intelligence' we must be careful not to start fooling ourselves overmuch that one thing is a direct measure of the other!

Before looking at attempts to measure intelligence, let us reflect on the relative merits of the exercise. (This is a matter to which we shall return.) IQ testing can be thought distasteful and useless. It can be intrusive, it can be poorly carried out, it can be wholly inappropriate in execution and in interpretation of results. Should it be scrapped, then? Some leading psychologists say it should (e.g. Stott, 1978b) and emphasise that we are committing a serious error in thinking that we can actually *measure* what is really no more than a *hypothetical construct*. This is to say, we make a conceptual leap from numbers and statistics to inferring some hypothetical psychological entity. But many academic and practising psychologists would disagree and argue that if we abandoned the practice of measuring intelligence then it would only be replaced by something equally as crude and inappropriate. The more balanced view taken by others (e.g. Heim, 1975 and Dockrell, 1970) is that when used with care it has considerable utility as a very useful tool in many educational and clinical situations. There are many educational problems to analyse and solve, and often these require very careful assessment. The only way one can recognise problems in some definable way, treat them and measure the results with any precision is to have criterion measures, and often, though not always, measures of intelligence are a useful aid in the total assessment process. What must be done is to strive to improve the criterion measures or to replace them with more innovatory methods, and to educate those who administer and interpret them. Scrapping the IQ may not solve any problems.

In this chapter the early history of mental measurement is briefly examined, and this is followed by an outline of 'conventional' tests used today. These tests have many serious limitations and disadvantages, and so after a brief examination of the major concepts involved in these measures, the various criticisms which have been raised are discussed. Some extremely interesting and promising innovatory work and methods are then examined, and the chapter is brought to a close with a summary embodying the major conclusions and implications for educators.

Early historical background

Psychological testing is a very young activity. The fundamental purposes are to measure differences between individuals' psychological processes, or to monitor any change within a single person over time, and also to find inter-relationships of these processes within the individual, the results often being used for purposes of prediction. How did it all begin? For an interesting collation of original research extracts, see Anastasi (1965).

Just around the turn of the century, early investigators looked at very elementary 'sensory' capacities in their attempts to research individual differences in intelligence. Work on the smallest sound pitch differences, the reaction time to respond to flashing lights (Galton, 1883) and the learning of nonsense syllables (Ebbinghaus, 1897) are examples of early measures. This was an unpromising start. Investigators found that results bore little relationship to students' work, and the tests did not really gel—student X could be very good on one and poor on another.

The first real breakthrough in measuring individual differences which relate to educational matters was the achievement of Alfred Binet. He and his co-workers criticised the sensory tests as being too simple, and thought more complex processes should be monitored—aspects of comprehension, judgment, and reasoning are reflected in Binet's definition of intelligence (chapter 1). He had been working along these lines when in 1904 the French Minister of Public Instruction asked him to study the problem of mental retardation in Parisian schools. The impetus to mental measurement came largely from a desire to identify and thereby classify the mentally deficient. As a response to the government request, Binet and Simon in 1905 published the first scale, utilising more complex psychological functions, which gave an overall index of intellectual level. This 1905 scale contained thirty items (or questions) such as execution of simple commands, verbal knowledge of objects, ability to define words, knowledge of pictures and completion of sentences. They were designed for use with children from three years upwards. The wide range of mental functions sampled were summarised by Binet in a very new concept—that of Mental Age (MA). Binet actually took the idea from earlier writers, and he applied it as a revolutionary way of allocating mental status to children of varying chronological (or actual physical) age (CA). The majority of, say, five-year-olds would manage the items on the five-year-old level—the Mental Age of five. Thus, if a seven-year-old could only successfully manage the five-year-old level, and failed the sixth, seventh level, etc., then although his CA = 7, his MA = 5.

Can intelligence be measured?

This proved to be a wonderful new psychological/educational toy! From these early beginnings the flood-gates opened. The Scale was revised in 1908 and in 1911 by Binet, and in 1916 Terman at Stanford University in the USA revised it substantially. Further revisions took place in 1937 and 1960. The Stanford-Binet is still used extensively today as an individual test by qualified psychologists. The story is a fascinating one, often horrific, and has been well documented elsewhere (Wolf, 1973; Butcher, 1968; Sattler, 1974).

With the birth and development of the Binet Scales came the associated birth of more ugly notions. The useful notion of MA was utilised by Binet, and is still utilised in the modern Stanford-Binet instrument. The ugliness came in other guises not attributable to Binet. For example, the idea that the scales were measuring innate intelligence, and that the MA measures were fixed for all time in early school life became popular views. The notion of using, MA and CA in a fraction form (or ratio, or quotient) was launched by Stern (1914) and this was known as the Intelligence Quotient (IQ). The formula he devised was:

$$\text{Intelligence Quotient (IQ)} = \frac{\text{Mental Age (MA)}}{\text{Chronological Age (CA)}} \times 100$$

Binet reacted strongly to what be called the 'brutal pessimism' enshrined in these sorts of doctrines and beliefs, and had he not died prematurely in 1911 one wonders how the next fifty years of mental testing would have differed.

Around this period, Spearman was developing his influential theory of 'g'—general ability. It was held that the individually administered Binet Scales gave a measure of 'g'. What now was required were quicker group tests of 'g', and the first was designed by Otis in 1916. This contained easy to difficult items for comprehension (analogies, opposites, etc.) and a form of this is still in use today. It was the American involvement in the First World War which gave group testing a boost. A quick method was required to sort out the general ability of 1¾ million men and the Army Alpha (for those who could read) and the Army Beta (a symbols test for the illiterate) proved to be high predictors of efficiency at a variety of Army jobs. What else would sort through, classify and select millions of men so efficiently and so quickly?

It was but a small step to apply those procedures to the school situation. In the years following the First World War Ballard (1922) and

Burt (1921) amongst others, designed tests of scholastic ability and achievement and in the 1930s the famous Moray House Scholarship tests were launched.

Why the popularity? In short, because the tests which sampled inter-related, complex intellectual skills were good selectors and predictors—they proved very efficient at selecting, classifying and allocating people to convenient tasks, boxes, categories; they seemed to predict before the start of something how successful the outcome would be. A pertinent example is the history of the eleven-plus selection tests. Like it or not, such a simple procedure did allow administrators to select and classify children for various types of education (grammar, secondary modern) and those who did well in GCE examinations at sixteen years were, on the whole, those who scored high marks in the eleven-plus procedures earlier. There are many issues here to which we shall return, but the apparent efficiency and success of such mental measurement largely accounts for the historical popularity.

Many other measures were devised, most of which are still in use today. Some of these will be considered in the next section.

Modern conventional tests (norm-referenced measures)

'Conventional' refers to the so-called 'norm-referenced' measures. There are literally hundreds available at the present time which can be administered on a group or individual basis, and which broadly phrase questions in verbal, non-verbal, or mixed forms. Let us deal with these ideas one at a time.

A norm-referenced measure is a test that allocates the testee to some ordinal rank, or position. The test score indicates how X performed in relation to everyone else on which the test was standardised. In constructing a test, the makers select the items that make up the questions and the population in which they are interested (e.g. five- to nine-year olds; or the adult population). These decisions depend on various criteria (see, for example, Butcher, 1968). The test is then given to a representative *sample* of the target population and the raw scores put through a statistical procedure. This results in comparable standard scores for all who eventually take the test. This, broadly, is what is meant by a standardised test. It is norm-referenced: norms are provided and one can compare X's score with that of the rest of the relevant population—is his score average, or lower than the average, etc.

The score often tells us little about the actual skills required to get to this position in the population—its main function is to classify an individual as bright, average, dull, etc., and these terms by definition are relative, not absolute.

Associated with this standardisation process are some central concepts which we briefly discuss below—for a more extensive treatment, see further reading. The normal distribution curve is a bell-shaped curve which summarises the nature of the distribution of IQ scores (see figure 2.1 and table 2.1).

Standardised scores	70	85	100	115	130	145
Standard deviations	−2	−1	0	1	2	3

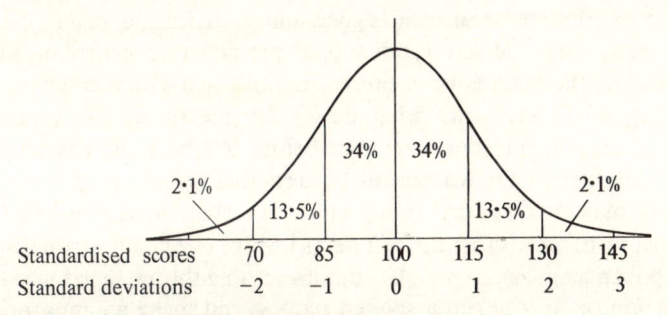

Figure 2.1 The normal distribution curve

It indicates that a few people do either well or badly on a test and most congregate around the average relative to each other. The average, or mean is arbitrarily allocated a score of 100 and the scores are arranged to fall away from this mean in a pre-determined fashion. The standard deviation is a measure which describes such scatter or variation, in scores above and below the mean—this is often arbitrarily fixed at 15 points for most tests (see figure 2.1). Thus the scores on modern IQ tests are deviation scores, or standard scores which are raw scores from tests converted to a standard scale by obeying the laws of the normal curve (hence the expression norms). Test scores are never thought to be perfectly accurate because each time an individual takes a test, factors may be operating which will artifically affect his levels of performance (e.g. not feeling particularly well on the test occasion). An account is taken for this error by using a standard error of measurement for each test. Basically, this tells us that any score obtained will be expected to vary within a few points on each test occasion—e.g. an IQ test may have a standard error of 4 points, so that a score of 110 should really be viewed as a range: 106–114 (110±4).

This last point refers to the fact that measurement by tests cannot be made with perfect accuracy. Test error is bound to occur, but this is allowable only within certain limits. The term used to describe this variation in error is test reliability. Within the expected degree of variation (as expressed by the standard error), test scores should be consistent, and fairly stable—they should be reliable.

Tests should also be valid—the makers of a test should be able to demonstrate that their test is actually measuring what they claim it is measuring. For example, a test of reading 'comprehension' should actually measure this, and not something else like simple recognition skills—if X scores high it must be because he is understanding what he reads. and not because he is good only at 'barking at print'. There are many forms of test validity (e.g. predictive, concurrent, etc.). However, the main issue at present in this discussion is to know the validity of IQ tests—just what are IQ tests measuring. We return to this important question later, but before this we must continue to describe further the features of IQ tests themselves.

The major ways of presenting a test are verbal and non-verbal. The verbal form means that the test items involve essentially written and/or spoken language. Generally, this means that the testee has to read a question or to listen to a spoken request and make an appropriate response. The verbal scores are the most highly associated with scholastic achievement and are often seen as measures of general scholastic ability. Verbal intelligence scores are very good predictors of success in academic studies. But there is a sting in this particular tail which we shall examine shortly. How can we assess the reasoning ability of those who cannot read and/or are not too proficient in understanding spoken language—e.g. immigrant children or children who seem to have poor social and linguistic backgrounds? One way is to present items non-verbally, with as little language involved as is possible. This can be accomplished by using pictures and symbols, which tap a type of thinking not essentially requiring language. Figure 2.2 shows examples of tests (see Vernon, 1960 for further examples).

Tests are designed primarily for group or individual administration. Group tests are not usually suitable for children below seven years of age. Above seven they are essentially only able to provide very rough indications of mental functioning. For a more precise assessment, an individual measure should be used. Apart from any other consideration, the individual test does allow the examiner to observe the emotional responses and attitudes of the individual child as well as providing a more detailed test score. Two major individual tests

Can intelligence be measured? 27

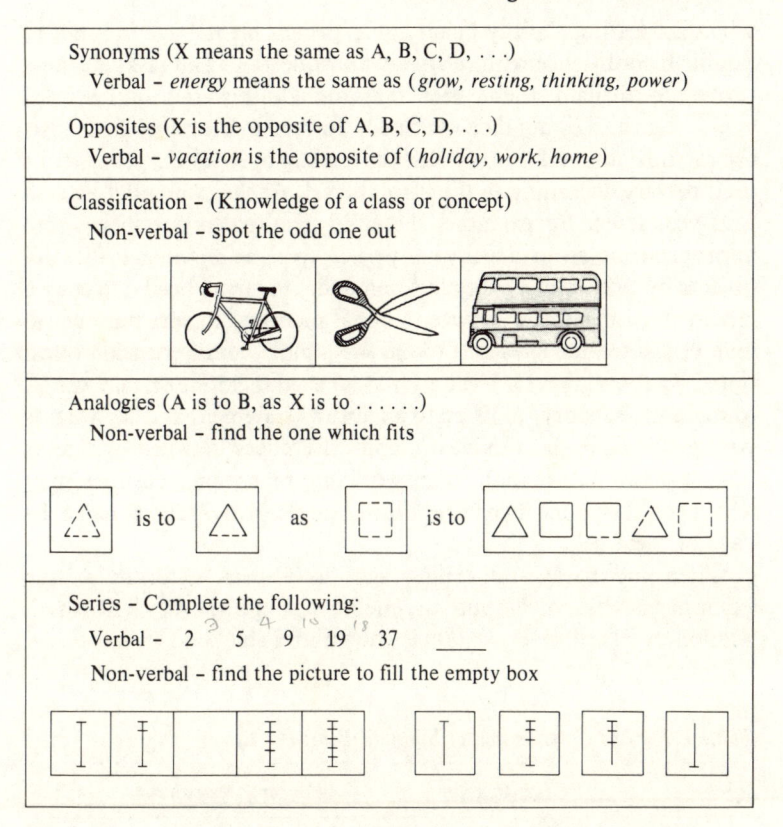

Synonyms (X means the same as A, B, C, D, ...)   Verbal - *energy* means the same as (*grow, resting, thinking, power*)
Opposites (X is the opposite of A, B, C, D, ...)   Verbal - *vacation* is the opposite of (*holiday, work, home*)
Classification - (Knowledge of a class or concept)   Non-verbal - spot the odd one out
Analogies (A is to B, as X is to ......)   Non-verbal - find the one which fits
Series - Complete the following: Verbal - 2 5 9 19 37   Non-verbal - find the picture to fill the empty box

Figure 2.2 Examples of items from group verbal and non-verbal tests. (Examples are fictitious, but are similar to material actually used.) The test can either provide a series of possible answers from which one must be chosen (called multiple-choice) or the testee has to provide an answer with no such help.

used by educational and clinical psychologists are briefly described below. These are the Stanford-Binet and the Wechsler tests.

The Stanford-Binet intelligence scale

The tests originally developed by Binet underwent several revisions in the USA. The latest used in Great Britain is the 1960 (1972 norms) revision, which is suitable for children aged two-and-a-half years and upwards. No one child testee is required to try all items; the examiner will start testing slightly below the expected mental age in order to establish confidence with relatively easy questions and tasks. If these prove too difficult, then easier items are administered until a 'basal age' is found. Testing then continues upward to a level when all tests are too difficult and this is called the 'ceiling age'. The types of items tend to vary according to the mental level. At the two-and-a-half- to four-year level, for example, the child is asked to put shapes into appropriate holes, to identify body parts, to name pictures, to identify objects by use, to obey simple commands, to string beads, to copy a circle, to discriminate between animal pictures, to sort buttons, to give opposite analogies and to answer simple comprehension questions. By the eight-year level, a child is asked to define certain words, to memorise a story, to listen to an absurd statement and say what is wrong, to name the similarities and differences between two items (e.g. football and apple), to answer comprehension questions (e.g. what should be done if you break someone else's toy?) and to name the days of the week.

When the basal and ceiling ages have been determined, the examiner is able to compute the mental age and the IQ. The classification of Stanford-Binet IQs is shown in Table 2.1

Table 2.1 The classification of Stanford-Binet IQ

IQ	Classification	Per cent of population
Above 139	Very superior	1·5
120–39	Superior	11
110–19	High average	18
90–109	Average	46
80–9	Low average	15
70–9	Borderline	6
Below 70	Mentally retarded	2·5

There have been many criticisms of the Stanford-Binet and we shall look briefly at two major ones.

Can intelligence be measured? 29

1 The easy items are well sprinkled with varied tasks—looking at pictures, performing practical tasks, answering questions and so on. However, these very soon give way to an almost total verbal battery of items. In the examples above, almost all of the eight-year-old level items have no equipment and all the items are entirely verbally stated questions and answers. This over-verbal approach tends to discriminate unfairly against certain children, and in particular against lower socio-economic groups. Binet never intended his scales to be a measure of narrow cognitive tasks, but utilised a much broader concept of intelligence.

2 A second criticism is that when all is done and computed, we are left essentially with a single number, the IQ. We have neither a very reliable way of finding strengths and weaknesses, nor are we able to use the results educationally (apart from the dubious classifications as shown in the Table 2.1). Sattler (1974) does, however, suggest ways of compiling a 'profile' of scores from the Stanford-Binet, but even this approach has been criticised—Akhurst (1970) notes that because test items are standardised in terms of the test as a whole, then it is not possible technically to compare an individual's results over the different kinds of items.

The Wechsler tests

Since the early 1940s, David Wechsler has been producing a series of instruments for the individual assessment of intelligence. As a result of his work, we have today the Wechsler Pre-school and Primary Scale of Intelligence (WPPSI) published in 1967 for use with children aged four to six-and-a-half years, the Wechsler Intelligence Scale for Children—Revised (WISC—R) published originally in 1949 and revised in 1974 for children aged six to sixteen years eleven months, and the Wechsler Adult Intelligence Scale (WAIS) published in 1955. All three scales have essentially the same format and organisation, although obviously the level of difficulty varies according to age level. These will be described generally below.

The main characteristics of Wechsler's scale are as follows:

1 The scales fall into two major categories: the verbal scale and the performance scale. These are comprised of a number of sub-tests (examples are fictitious):

The verbal scale tests measure levels of functioning using previously learned verbal material.

Information—questions tap the general range of information (e.g. 'How many minutes make an hour?')

Comprehension—tests practical information, the extent of personal responsibility assumed and the ability to evaluate past experience (e.g. 'What would you do if lost in a strange city?')

Arithmetic—verbal problems test arithmetic computation and reasoning (e.g. 'If I spent half of £1 how much would I have left?')

Similarities—measures conceptual reasoning—the testee is required to organise information to draw analogies (e.g. 'How are wheels and balls similar?')

Vocabulary—testee has to recall information in order to define words. Tests word knowledge (e.g. 'What is an aeroplane?')

Digit span—a series of numbers are spoken by the examiner (e.g. 7—6—8—3—5) and they must be repeated in a forward or reverse form. Tests short-term rote memory and attention.

The performance scale tests show how the testee fares with relatively new and novel material presented practically rather than verbally. Most of these items are timed, with bonus points for quick and successful performance.

Picture completion—the missing part of an incomplete picture must be named or pointed out; this tests visual alertness and visual memory; the child is allowed fifteen seconds for each picture.

Picture arrangement—comic-strip-type pictures must be arranged from a standard presentation to tell a story; this tests sequential thinking and the understanding of social situations.

Block design—pictures have been copied using multi-coloured blocks; this tests the ability to perceive and analyse patterns, and allows the tester to check for any problems of manipulation.

Object assembly—the jig-saw type puzzle must be assembled from a standard format; this tests the ability to deal with part-whole relationships.

Coding—numbers have to be associated with symbols; this tests speed of learning and writing (only two minutes allowed) and

Can intelligence be measured? 31

highlights any faults of short-term memory and sequential memory.

2 The results from these tests are presented as a verbal IQ, a performance IQ, and a full-scale IQ. In addition, for each area there is a profile of five or six sub-tests. An illustration of this is shown in figure 2.3. Thus, a fuller picture for intellectual ability is available indicating strengths and weaknesses, if any.

Verbal scale	Scaled scores
Information	9
Comprehension	6
Arithmetic	10
Similarities	13
Vocabulary	11
	49

Performance scale	
Picture completion	14
Picture arrangement	10
Block design	19
Object assembly	15
Coding	11
	69

Verbal score	= 49	Verbal IQ	= 100
Performance score	= 69	Performance IQ	= 127
Full scale score	= 118	Full IQ	= 114
		(not a simple average)	

Figure 2.3 Test score of a fourteen-year-old boy shown in record and profile form on the WISC-R

Note the discrepancies in performance across and within the two scales. This might be indicative of some important findings, and if so would be very useful educational information. It might, however, be an artificial finding due to chance and other less significant factors (see discussion in the text).

Any verbal-performance differences and any variations within each scale might indicate important factors to the psychologist. There are no simple rules to follow in this type of analysis, however. In general the psychologist uses this type of test as an exceptional opportunity to observe behaviour and thought processes.

Some writers have gone even further than this type of profile and indicate how more educational information can be devised from the results (e.g. Searls, 1975).

3 Wechsler discarded the original IQ equation and brought in the new idea of 'deviation' IQs based upon scaled scores. These were briefly explained earlier in this chapter. In figure 2.3 we see the scaled scores (which have been arrived at by comparing the subject's actual chronological age with his raw test scores) range from zero to nineteen. Ten is the average, and they are marked off from this in threes. This is because three is the standard deviation. This indicates that the majority of any age group will score between seven and thirteen ($+1$ and -1 standard deviations from the mean). Thus, any score below seven and above thirteen becomes more meaningful in these terms.

We can see, therefore, that Wechsler's tests look at a broad spectrum of mental ability and provide profiles based upon deviation IQ, and scaled scores. In fact, Wechsler refuses to regard intelligence in any unitary manner, but prefers rather to think in terms of a whole array of abilities which include such personality factors as persistence and drive. Beyond this broad rationale there is no real theory behind his tests—he just samples abilities which are thought to be important. No one ability is considered to have any greater or lesser status than any other. (Galton regarded this type of exercise as the exploratory sinking of shafts at carefully chosen points.) Where did Wechsler get his ideas for his tests—how did he arrive at these particular ten or eleven rather than others? Sattler (1974) argues that most of the contents are 'borrowed' from the Army Alpha, and Beta tests, the Stanford-Binet and other famous tests of the 1920–1930 period. Thus, the WISC-R, for instance, is largely derived from other tests, and in particular the Binet, for its content. All this criticism amounts to saying that we are just not sure what the Wechsler tests are actually measuring (the validity of the test is not proven). Like the Stanford-Binet, it is culturally loaded and tends to discriminate against lower socio-economic groups. It is also often difficult to see precisely how the profile of results can be utilised educationally, and some even criticise this very practice (e.g. Bijou, 1976). Brody and Brody (1976) are particularly critical of the use of the Wechsler scales in identifying strengths and weaknesses. They cogently argue that many 'qualified' psychologists do not understand the psychometric properties of the scales, and often draw some very misleading and invalid conclusions. This is due in part to a lack of understanding about the reliability of each of the ten or so sub-test scores—the reliabilities vary considerably and any differences across the profile might even be due to no more than chance factors and random fluctuations on a particular testing occasion.

On these grounds alone the Wechsler tests are hardly adequate, and thus far from perfect. However, they are technically amongst the most reliable and most thorough tests of intelligence that we possess at the moment. Wechsler admits to being a pragmatist—he does not think that his tests necessarily add up to 'intelligence', but prefers to think that intelligence is known by what it enables us to do (Wechsler, 1966). On this pragmatic basis, his measures should not be entirely dismissed.

Criticisms of conventional tests

Intelligence and ability tests are obviously measuring something, but the major problem is just what that something may be. This is a major criticism because if we are busy taking measurements with the type of instruments described in this chapter and if we are unsure of the validity of these tools, then making decisions about the future and educational provision for children is far short of the 'scientific' precision and confidence required.

So what are these tests measuring? First, most tests adopt deviation IQs, which are normalised standard scores with a mean of 100 and a standard deviation of usually 15 points. This means that IQ scores do not represent absolute measurements with a zero point, like height and weight. A test result only tells us what the child's status is in relation to all the other children who have taken the same test. When these scores are plotted on a graph they invariably result in a normal distribution curve. Now this curve can indicate at least two things—(i) that intelligence is itself normally distributed in the population and the tests are reflecting and confirming this fact of nature, or (ii) that the curve is a direct result of the kind of test items selected and the result is an artificial, made-up normal curve that is a fluke! In fact, most tests come under (ii)—they are constructed in order to ensure a normal distribution because the test makers make the assumption that intelligence is normally distributed. This assumption is criticised by some as being very dubious (e.g. Ryan, 1972; Bijou, 1976; Bloom, 1971). Such writers would argue that there is no good reason why test scores should not be distributed in a variety of ways, often depending on the type of cognitive skill under test. There is certainly no extremely sound evidence to lead us to assume that intelligence follows the rules of a mathematically determined normal curve.

But let us return to the actual tests themselves. What criteria are used in the selection of items for use in intelligence tests? The main ones are not as one might hope—based on a well-researched theoretical account of how children learn and develop with age, nor by how an item is developmentally significant for some stage of development. These criteria are seldom mentioned. Rather the main criteria for inclusion are statistical in nature—that items should show differences between age groups (so that the test discriminates well), that items correlate highly with the final score (test consistency) and that items provide similar results over re-testing periods (test reliability). Furthermore, if an IQ test as a whole is validated, it is usually done so against the external and supposedly independent criterion of school attainment—to ensure that the test is measuring what it is supposed to measure, a check is made against school performance. Those doing well at school should have the higher IQ results. Why should this be so? Even more disturbing is the tendency to use low IQ as a justification for low scholastic achievement/poor progress. It is apparent that IQ tests are measuring broad, generalised thinking skills, but this is a measure of the type of achievement just as a reading test is a measure of more narrower skills which have been acquired. These tests are not different in kind, only in degree (see chapter 5). What this amounts to is the so-called problem of 'psychological reality' of the psychometric approach—we have to make a conceptual leap from statistical results to inferring some psychological significance. The tests are assumed to sample underlying or latent ability, and this assumption of some form of 'real' existence stemming from numerical relationships is questionable. What makes it worse, as we have discussed, is the further assumption that the tests have some casual, explanatory status (see Gillham, 1978).

So when we actually find out how test questions are chosen, we find little relationship with the theoretical nature of intelligence (howsoever this is construed), nor with the views on how children learn and develop, and test items as a whole often appear to measure rather trivial aspects of behaviour. It is often difficult to interpret the results (even from the better, individually administered batteries) in an educationally useful way. Because of this, many professional psychologists see such tests as being largely irrelevant as investigatory tools, and prefer to use methods of looking at actual school behaviour and performance in school learning. Thus, if reading is the problem, then examine the reading skills of a child, and only when the use of an IQ test is considered really relevant to a case would one be used. Because the criteria discussed are statistical in nature, it is hardly surprising to find, for example, that IQs appear to be relatively stable for the majority of people (though by no means for all) and that they are highly correlated with school performance. They have been designed to produce such effects! In fact, there is 'an illusion of objectivity' as Ryan (1972) skilfully points out. It really is a most strange way of measuring cognitive development—each score can only be expressed as a function of the scores of others in the same age group because all an IQ really tells us is how far up the scale of difficulty an individual has progressed in relation to the rest of that age group!

Elliott (1976) discusses these problems and suggests a measurement model which overcomes many of the above difficulties. It is to these more innovatory techniques that we turn next.

But before we examine these techniques we must briefly note some less technical objections to the testing movement. These are important yet raise rather wide issues, and they revolve around sociological and phenomenological problems. Simon (1971) discusses the social processes of discrimination which lie behind the use of testing. The use of a test, it is argued, betrays certain values, ideology and the social position of the tester. The result often becomes a process of alienation. Simon (1971) argues that 'the administration of tests, with the aim of achieving the finest degree of accuracy in differentiating children, had a good deal more to do with ideas in the heads of teachers than potentialities in children'. He brings together critiques from branches of sociology, history and politics in attacking the notion that 'school systems run on the assumption that no child could ever rise above himself, that his level of achievement was fatally determined by an I.Q.' (Simon, 1971). On a related note, phenomenologists would question what the mental testers would take for granted, and argue that there is no such thing as 'objective' tests. All information and data are essentially personal reconstructions, reflecting our intentions and purposes. This is a very different approach to the passive and deterministic ideology adopted by the psychometricians, and the phenomenologists would plea for a more 'natural' approach to evaluation, in general (see Hamilton, et al., 1977).

Innovations in mental measurement (criterion-referenced and diagnostic measures)

Norm-referenced tests tend to remove testing from teaching—it is often difficult to know what a score means, how it can inform actual teaching activities and often does little to guide teaching and curriculum content. Although this is not always the case, there is more than a grain of truth in this criticism. For a cogent discussion of these points, see Kiernan and Jones (1977).

Ideally a test should tell something about strengths and weaknesses of a child's thinking. It should be diagnostic. Many attainment tests available to teachers do just this—and on the information provided by the results, competent teachers are able to alter their teaching in some way to help surmount a difficulty that the assessment has highlighted. But are we able to do this for more general reasoning and thinking? We are able to discover that a child is 'not very bright', possibly with an IQ of 80, say, and that most of his classmates have higher scores. But can we say just what is making his score lower than the others, and can we use this information to try to teach him more efficient ways of reasoning and thinking? Some of the above mentioned individual tests go some way toward this, as for example with the profiles provided by the Wechsler scales (though these are restricted tests, only for the use of qualified psychologists).

The innovations in this field which are in the very early and elementary stages of development are those of criterion-referenced measures of ability. For a full discussion see Ward (1970) and Hambleton *et al.* (1978). A criterion-referenced test sets out to help the teaching process directly. It is not concerned with relative performance (how X compares with the rest of his age group) but rather with finding out whether or not X is able to do a named and defined task or not (called the criterion task). Glaser (1963) states that the notion of the continuum of knowledge acquisition ranging from no proficiency to perfect performance is at the base of this approach, along with that of sequential, hierarchical learning. A hierarchy of skill is drawn up in some defined area. Each point in the hierarchy can only successfully be accomplished if those items below have been mastered. Thus, in order to add up numbers, one has to be competent in 'lower' skills such as recognising digits, counting, etc. Criterion-reference tests, then, ideally provide information as to level of skill competence acquired, and inform the teacher where to start teaching. Scores provide explicit information as to what an individual can/cannot do.

Can intelligence be measured? 37

(This is related to Hunt's 'problem of the match' which is discussed in chapter 5.) As Leach and Raybould (1977) and Stones (1969) note, the question of objectives is the crux of this matter, and this is discussed in chapter 5.

Experimental work

If intelligence is hierarchically organised, a question we look at again in chapter 4, then the nature of this hierarchy will guide an assessment strategy. Such a strategy has been formulated by Uzgiris and Hunt (1975) for the first two years of life and by Hunt and Kirk (1974) for the period from two to early school years, although the work is still very much in an infantile, if not embryonic state! Possible developments in the future are, however, very exciting—the benefits of advancement here, educationally speaking, would be enormous.

Uzgiris and Hunt (1975) have attempted to write criterion-referenced measures for the assessment of intellectual functioning in infancy (first two years, roughly). They adopt ordinal scales of behaviour based on a hierarchy of development following largely the developmental psychology of Jean Piaget (see chapter 4). The achievements of an infant at one point in his development are based on those skills which were developed earlier and which have been incorporated into the present, more complicated abilities. This is a very different concept from that of the MA. The MA/IQ score is found usually by adding up all the correct items passed. It does not distinguish in any way between the relationship between what a child is able to do at one level from another level. Getting a higher score simply means that more items were passed. Uzgiris and Hunt, however, have designed ordinal scales to describe a young infant in terms of the level of organisation in each of six areas or branches of development. These consist of the development of visual pursuit, the development of means for obtaining desired events, the development of imitation (vocal and gestural), the development of causality, how objects relate in space, and the development of schemas for relating to objects. Table 2.2 shows one scale in more detail. These scales have been used successfully, for example, in assessing the intelligence of preschool mentally handicapped children (ESN-S). See Stevens (1976). The psychologist can ascertain carefully in which behaviours on the scales the child shows competence, and where the child apparently lacks competence. This, roughly, is the point at which direct teaching should commence, because the future development, if it is arranged hierarchically, can be based upon established foundations. The strategy, at least, is both better than intuitive trial and error guesswork, and is geared to the educational needs of the child.

Table 2.2 *Example of a scale for examining the development of object schemas* (based on Uzgiris and Hunt, 1975)

Behaviour displayed (schemas)	Objects given to infant (examples)					
	Rattle	Doll	Cup	Bell	Beads	...
Holds object						
Mouths object						
Inspects object						
Hits with object						
Shakes object						
More complex examination						
Drops object						
Throws object						
Uses object socially (e.g. drinks, builds, sniffs)						
Shows object						
Names object						

Such a behaviour scale as this is based on a functional hierarchy of responses; it assesses increasingly complex sequences of action and levels of symbolic representation. The tester watches carefully what the infant does with each single object as it is presented, and records the behaviour on the response sheet.

Hunt and Kirk (1974) were concerned to develop criterion-referenced measures of intellectual functioning for school readiness tasks. Their work begins to take up where Uzgiris and Hunt leave off. They make similar hierarchical assumptions, saying that in order for a child to benefit from tasks normally required in an admissions class, a child needs to possess some basic intellectual competences. Their tests were designed to see whether or not these skills have been acquired. If not, then the teaching and required tasks must be altered accordingly. They focused on 'representational competence' by which they mean that the language and thought processes of the child have to be integrated to allow for future intellectual development. Hunt noted that teachers in admissions classes generally assume that children 'understand the words for such perceptual abstractions as colour, position, shape and number, have words for them in their vocabulary, and can easily communicate such information'. But this is not generally the case with children from poor and disadvantaged families. These children, Hunt claims, probably fail in school not because they are poor learners, but because they are being asked to do things way above their present levels of competence and understanding. Although not considered to be the only skill areas of importance, Hunt and Kirk designed the following four criterion-referenced tests:

1 Test for the identification of colour;
2 Test for the identification of position;
3 Test for the identification of shapes;
4 Test for the identification of numbers of objects.

Each of these tests took more or less the same format, and number (1) is described for illustration.

The materials for the colour identification test consists of a white board on which are glued six one-inch cubes in red, orange, yellow, green, brown and blue. The child is seated at a table and the examiner places the board in front of him.

The first stage of the test is perceptual identification. The examiner says 'Look what we have here' and guides the child's finger to touch each of the cubes. He then places a loose blue block on top of the fixed blue one and says. 'This one goes here'. This is repeated for all of the colours. The loose blocks are then removed and he asks the child to put the blocks back to where they belong. After one trial the board is reversed and a second trial is carried out.

The second stage is spoken identification. The examiner puts his finger on a block and says, 'What colour is this block?' and so on through all the colours. The board is reversed and a second trial administered.

The third stage is listening identification. The child is asked to 'Touch the blue block' and so on through all the colours and again the board is reversed for a second trial.

Essentially, this same procedure is followed for the other tests—for example, for position, the moves are: putting things on, under, in front of, between, and so on. So the examiner is evaluating the skills of imitation (first stage), naming, or encoding (second stage), and recognising names of decoding (third stage).

Hunt and Kirk compared pre-school children from middle-class families with children from poorer families who were taking part in a compensatory project called 'Headstart' (see chapter 3). They found that as the level of difficulty increased, then both groups scored more errors. However, this error increase was far more pronounced for the Headstart children. For the colour test, for instance, 83 per cent of Headstart children performed perfectly on both trials of perceptual identification (as compared with 100 per cent middle class children), 24 per cent for spoken identification (76 per cent middle) and 19 per cent for listening identification (90 per cent middle). These are large differences and are obviously important information for the teacher when children enter school. These central skills which children need in the reception class vary considerably according to the quality of previous experiences, and the curriculum must be designed and adapted accordingly.

These measures tell us in part where to start teaching. They are very practical. An ordinary IQ type measure would have told us much less than this. With further research this area of intellectual assessment seems very promising indeed, to say the least. In one sense, the approach is nearer in spirit to the 'mini learning experiment' advocated by Leach and Raybould (1977) which is discussed in chapters 1 and 5. What this approach really amounts to is that we are getting nearer to using our knowledge of how children learn and develop in the assessment of their cognitive skills, and relying less on more artificial statistically based assessments. There is a place for both, of course. A new measure which combines both approaches is now discussed.

British Ability Scales (BAS)

Another very innovatory battery to assess intelligence and make individual cognitive evaluations are the British Ability Scales (1978). The development team under Colin Elliot at Manchester University have adopted a very new and promising approach to individual assessment which is related to the notion of criterion-referenced measurement. There are twenty-four scales which provide a wide range of opportunity to assess different abilities varying from reasoning to basic achievement (see tables 2.3 and 2.4). This allows the educational psychologist to assess with great flexibility children in the two- to seventeen-year-old range and provides (better than ever) opportunities to assess psychological processes with the educational implications firmly in mind. Technically the details are difficult to grasp (see Elliot, 1975, 1976 for further information) but the following advantages are built into the BAS because of a new statistical procedure called Rasch scaling:

(a) Abilities may be estimated which are norm-free, that is criterion-based, allowing direct estimates of a particular ability to be made—instead of saying how X compares with the relevant population, we are told how his skills fare on this or that scale. We are then in a much stronger position educationally to decide what, if anything, should be done.

(b) Ability estimates are sample-free and therefore similar to physical measurements—this generates many practical advantages, such as allowing flexible testing procedures, 'tailor-made' for particular individuals.

(c) New types of profiles are provided (technically referred to as expectancy tables) which evaluate the significance of any discrepancy between scores on different scales—that is the profile compares the differences across a number of scales with the individual testee in mind (not a population type profile comparison as with the WISC-R). In other words, the individual sets his own norms and more meaningful educational decisions can thus be made. This overcomes the serious technical difficulties associated with the interpretation of profiles as previously mentioned.

(d) The BAS is partly based on theoretical accounts of development, notably Piaget's work on number and on formal reasoning and on Kohlberg's work on moral development (called in the BAS Social Reasoning). In addition it incorporates a measure of speed of processing information which to an extent meets Eysenck's (1967) objection to normal measures.

What does this amount to? Many serious limitations of conventional tests were noted earlier in this chapter. What needs to be done to overcome these problems? As Elliot (1976) points out, if scales of development could be constructed that were (i) not dependent on a particular reference group, (ii) independent of specific items used in the test, (iii) where scores resemble physical measurements like height, and (iv) where one single scale covered the full range of ability and development, then those scales would be 'scarcely recognizable' in comparison with ordinary IQ measures. The BAS incorporates these significant advantages, though no doubt those who have a strong disinclination to 'test' will raise problems with the BAS as they have done with more conventional instruments—see discussion above and, for example, Gillham (1978).

Table 2.3 Classification of the twenty-four British Ability Scales, with their appropriate age range in years. (Reproduced with kind permission of Dr Colin Elliott et al. and the NFER Publishing Company Ltd, Windsor.)

	Principal stimulus mode>	Visual		Verbal	
	Principal response mode>	Motor	Verbal	Motor	Verbal
V Processes	Speed	Speed of information processing (8–17)			
Reasoning		Matrices (5–17)	Formal operation thinking (8–17)		Similarities (5–17) Social reasoning (5–17)
Spatial imagery	Accuracy	Rotation of letter-like forms (8–14) Visualisation of cubes (8–17) Block design (level) (4–17)			
	Accuracy & speed	Block design (power) (4–17)			
Perceptual matching		Matching letter-like forms (5–14) Copying (4–8)		Verbal-tactile matching (2½–8)	
Short-term memory	Recall immediate	Recall of designs (5–17)	Immediate visual recall (5–17)		Recall of digits (2½–17)
	delayed		Delayed visual recall (5–17)		
	Recognition	Visual recognition (2½–8)			
Retrieval and application of knowledge	Verbal accuracy		Naming vocabulary (2½–8) Word reading (5–14)	Verbal comprehension (2½–8)	Word definitions (5–17)
	quantity		Verbal fluency (4–17)		Verbal fluency (4–17)
	Numerical	Early number skills (2½–8) Basic arithmetic (5–14)			

Table 2.4 Selected examples of the processes measured by the BAS

Process	Sub-scale	Age	Task required
Reasoning	Matrices	5–17	Complete a pattern by drawing the correct design
	Similarities	5–17	Given three words from a class (of, e.g. fruit) provide a fourth and name the class
	Social reasoning	5–17	Evaluate verbally presented 'moral' problems
Spatial imagery	Block design	4–17	Construct patterns using black and yellow blocks
	Rotation of letter-like forms	8–14	Visualise how a letter-like figure would look when viewed from the opposite direction
Perceptual matching	Copying	4–8	Copy designs and letter-like forms
	Verbal-tactile matching	2½–8	From a verbal description, find objects inside a bag using hands only.
Short-term memory	Recall of designs	5–17	After a five-second presentation, draw a design from memory.
	Visual recall (Immediate/Delayed)	5–17	Recall drawings of objects (immediately and twenty minutes later)
	Visual recognition	2½–8	After seeing a drawing, find it when mixed in with others.
Retrieval and application of knowledge	Naming vocabulary	2½–8	Name objects shown
	Word reading	5–14	Read and define words— twenty-one are common to both scales (enabling useful comparisons)
	Word definition	5–17	
	Verbal comprehension	2½–8	Carry out operations in response to verbal commands
	Verbal fluency	4–17	Carry out 'creativity' type items

Basic arithmetic	5–14	Compute using the four rules
Early number skills	2½–8	Count and grade objects by size

In practice, the psychologist using the BAS will be able to select from the twenty-four scales those which are considered by him to be appropriate for the individual child under investigation, and will do so with the confidence of knowing that many of the criticisms of conventional measures have been largely overcome. Moreover, for the first time he will know that the test battery has been designed and standardised for a British population of children, and many of the scales are educationally much more meaningful as a basis for future curriculum planning—for example, measures of memory, matching letter-like forms, word reading, early number skills, verbal fluency (a crude measure of 'creative' skill) formal operational thinking, and moral/social reasoning. When a teacher asks 'What can I do in practical terms for this child?', the psychologist will be in a much stronger position to provide a useful answer.

Illinois Test of Psycholinguistic Abilities (ITPA)

As we have seen, most conventional tests of intelligence have been used mainly as classificatory instruments—single, global scores allow classification into broad categories for placement purposes. This has been referred to as *inter*-individual differences and variability. But diagnostic measures are concerned with strengths and weaknesses within the child—they are thus primarily *intra*-individual in their orientation. The ITPA is a diagnostic intra-individual test of psychological and linguistic functions (largely concerned therefore with the intellectual and cognitive processes in learning and development) and test results from this instrument can be used to plan remedial activities and programmes for those children who are requiring specific help in these processes. It is concerned with the specific cognitive abilities of children (in the two-and-a-half- to ten-year range) which are involved in communication, as well as a test of intelligence. It is based on an information processing model designed by Kirk based upon Osgood's work (1957). The model attempts to relate a set of functions whereby the intentions of one person are communicated to another, and functions which deal with the reception and interpretation of information. In short, this is referred to as psycholinguistic skill.

Essentially, this model relates three sets of cognitive dimensions: (1) psycholinguistic processes, (2) levels of organisation, and (3) channels of communication.

Can intelligence be measured? 45

1 The processes are involved with the acquisition and use of language whereby a child becomes able to receive, recognise and understand information. He is also able to 'do something with it' in his head in order to 'think'—concept formation, use of linguistic symbols and so on. Then in order to communicate and express his ideas, intentions, wishes, etc., he has to be able to respond by gesture or vocally.

2 This can happen at two levels—an automatic level where integrated and organised habits like memory, rote learning, etc., are involved, and at a more complex level where symbolic representation is involved.

PROCESSES

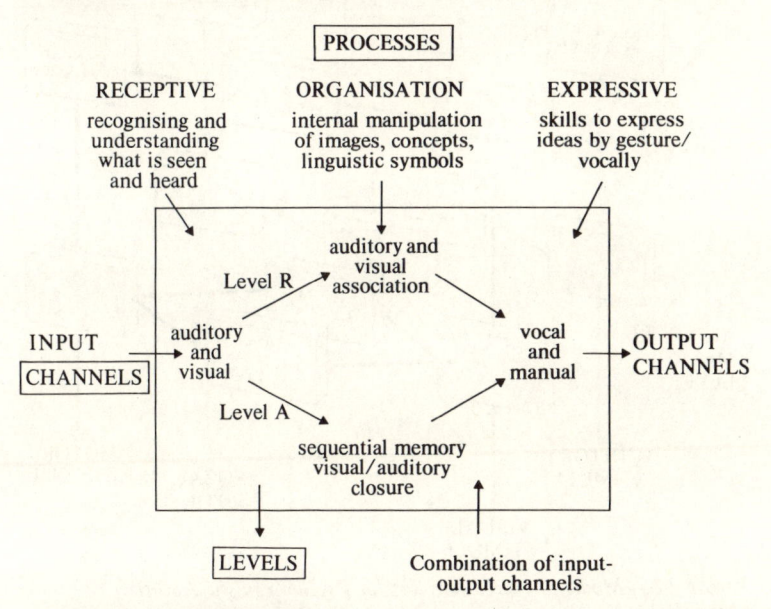

RECEPTIVE	ORGANISATION	EXPRESSIVE
recognising and understanding what is seen and heard	internal manipulation of images, concepts, linguistic symbols	skills to express ideas by gesture/vocally

INPUT CHANNELS → [Level R: auditory and visual association; auditory and visual; Level A: sequential memory visual/auditory closure; vocal and manual] → OUTPUT CHANNELS

LEVELS   Combination of input-output channels

Figure 2.4 Simplified model of the ITPA
R = Representative: use of symbols which carry meaning of objects, events, etc.
A = Automatic: habits of memory, rote learning, etc.

3 The routes through which the contents of communication flow are called channels and those principally involved at input are the visual and auditory modes (the senses of hearing and seeing), at output they are the motor and vocal modes (responding by doing or saying) and two major combinations of input-output of auditory-vocal and visual-motor are also involved.

A simple version of this model is shown in figure 2.4 and the model itself in figure 2.5. The results from this test are directly linked to

46 Can intelligence be measured?

remedial programmes, and some curriculum projects have been designed around the ITPA—the 'GOAL' language kit, marketed in the UK by Learning Development Aids, is especially useful for the design of individual programmes of work (language and associated skills) for young mentally handicapped children.

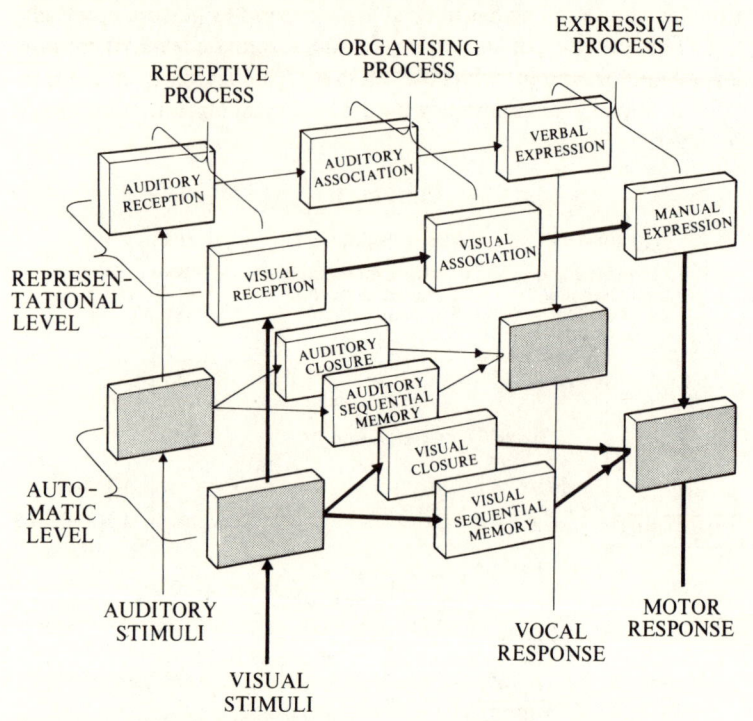

Figure 2.5 Model of the Illinois Test of Psycholinguistic Abilities (After J. N. Paraskevopoulos and S. A. Kirk, *The Development and Psychometric Characteristics of the Revised Illinois Test of Psycholinguistic Abilities*, University of Illinois Press, Chicago, 1969, p. 13. Reproduced with kind permission of the University of Illinois Press, Chicago.)

The ITPA has not been without its critics, however. Hammill and Larsen (1974) and Newcomer and Hammill (1975) note its conceptual and psychometric weaknesses. For example, the ITPA suffers from a defect, in common with other 'profile' type tests (but not the BAS), in that the sub-tests which indicate strengths and weaknesses stand up to close scrutiny only for large numbers. Although the overall score is technically satisfactory for any single child under investigation, the profile is not so sound as it might appear to be. A six-point difference, for example, may mean very little. This is because the reliabilities of each sub-test are not as high as they ought to be. (See Paraskevopoulos and Kirk, 1969). The validity of the ITPA has also been questioned—does it provide a comprehensive or relevant analysis of language skill? Some see it as too 'reductionist'—that is in splitting language up into these components (as in figure 2.5) we are perhaps in no better position to evaluate the ability. Some children might score poorly on certain components and yet present no serious problems in school learning, for example. Indeed, this has been a criticism levelled generally at the psychometric paradigm. But the ITPA is a very pragmatic instrument, based upon psycholinguistic principles of learning and development, and has generated much thinking, research and remedial programme writing over the last few years (see Kirk and Kirk, 1971; Paraskevopoulos and Kirk, 1969). One can only suppose that a similar programme of activity awaits the BAS.

Conclusions

In chapter 1 we discussed various views of intelligence—one was that intelligence is largely a single matter, as embodied in the notion of 'g'; another view, although not discounting 'g' (because most cognitive tests are positively intercorrelated) preferred to approach intelligence as an open, polymorphous concept. We attempted to specify this by referring to a number of highly developed skills which might constitute intelligent behaviour.

We have seen in this chapter how these two perspectives have been manifested, in part, in certain measures—group and individual tests of 'g' plus other factors, which really serve to classify people into categories (dull, gifted, etc.). It must be emphasised that these types of measures are only aspects of some elusive process which we call 'intelligence'. There are some major drawbacks in such tests, as discussed. Moreover, they are not a measure of innate intelligence (Intelligence A), nor are they direct measures of intelligent behaviour (Intelligence B). They are *samples* of 'B'—and there are occasions when careful decisions based on such measures might be educationally useful. This is because such tests sample broadly based measures of learning and thinking based on general experience. We must stress again that interpretation of single IQ figures needs to be made with the greatest caution and care.

Probably of much more use educationally are the criterion-referenced measures which examine specific skills involved in intelligence. We return to these in chapters 4 and 5.

Chapter 3

What affects intelligence?

Some important issues

There are no simple answers to the question 'What affects intelligence?', and never can be. The whole issue is riddled with complexity. Beginners often find this complexity quite bewildering, so here we present some starting-points and ideas on a very fundamental and greatly simplified level. The aim is to put this topic into a reasonably understandable format such that a beginner may read further references (which are often quite difficult) with some confidence.

We are using the term intelligence at this point to refer mainly to intelligence B (present levels of performance) and measures of it (IQ), although in parts the discussion will have implications for intelligence A (a person's biological potential). The issue of which factors, if any, affect these various meanings of intelligence is really quite central at this point in the book. In one way this chapter (and the next) are bridges which link the more theoretical aspects with the more applied and practical aspects of intelligence, as for example with areas of schooling and pre-schooling. For example, we earlier touched upon certain issues such as: are intelligence and learning closely related in development; does a child learn to develop a range of skills which enable him to cope with his environment; is the IQ fixed from birth; do we need to recognise certain inadequacies in measures of intelligence; are IQ tests a kind of achievement test, and so on? Thus, we now need to grasp a few nettles and ask just which factors are able to be named which might be involved in partly resolving these questions.

The issue of which factors affect intelligence is also very important for other immensely important reasons. We are really asking questions like 'What determines the competence of people? Is this fixed and immutable at birth or does it change with time and circumstances? If so, what circumstances foster maximum growth?' Now these types of questions are not just for academics and students preparing an essay or for an examination. They are questions of immense educational, social and not least political significance (see Simon, 1971). For example, if we were to decide that intelligence was fixed from birth and few factors could be manipulated to alter this, then a teacher might decide that only bright children should be stretched (a poor interpretation of streaming), a social worker might decide that there was little point in trying to improve the lot of inadequate families, and a politician at best might decide that it was pointless spending millions of pounds on pre-school building and at worst decide to sterilise the subnormal (or advocate types of eugenic and genetic engineering). None of these possibilities is beyond belief, and many people today still have such thoughts lingering at the back of their minds, not so much because they are 'wicked' but because they are ignorant of the research reported over the last few years.

One issue has been rumbling away in psychology for many, many years, and in essence what we have said so far in this chapter can be seen as one aspect of this debate: that of 'nature' or 'nurture'. Historically the arguments have run that either nature determines an individual's characteristics (IQ, personality, etc.), that person being born with them, and that's that; *or* characteristics are developed over time, starting as it were with a blank slate and that experience chalks in particular skills. These arguments (see Anastasi, 1958) are really emphasising mechanisms, or factors which lie, crudely 'inside' or 'outside' of a human being (body + CNS + brain). Very broadly, the various terms which are often used in such debates are summarised here, though the terms in each column do NOT share identical meanings.

Terms used in the nature/nurture debate

Inside	Outside
Nature	Nurture
Heredity	Environment
Genes/genetics	Psycho-social
Biological	Cultural
Maturation	Learning
Urges from within	Urges from without

Certain psychologists, notably Jensen and Eysenck, are prepared to state categorically that in matters such as intelligence, IQ scores are

80 per cent determined by the inside factors, and 20 per cent determined by the outside factors—if correct, a very pessimistic outlook indeed. However, the majority of scientists do not go along with these views partly for two reasons: (i) due to a theoretical disagreement; and (ii) due to the poor evidence usually given to substantiate the claims. These points will be discussed during the course of the chapter, and it is probably sufficient to make two points here: (a) that both inside and outside factors are crucial for the development of intellectual skills, since both sets are interacting—one set causing a change in the other, and vice versa; and (b) we should avoid saying which, proportionally, is more important and rather concentrate on what can actually be done in stimulating children's growth in intellectual competence.

So let us move on now to examine briefly some of these factors and see what is meant by 'inside' and 'outside'. There have been many reviews of such factors—e.g. Vernon, 1969, 1976a and 1976b; Rutter and Madge, 1976; Bronfenbrenner and Mahoney, 1975; Brody and Brody, 1976; Pilling and Pringle, 1978, etc. It would be very wrong to see these as working and operating individually, or to state categorically that one factor was more important than another. The object of this examination is to provide clues as to how one might improve levels of functioning, but we must bear in mind throughout that each factor is interacting with others—A may affect the operation of X, Y and Z (and thus change them) and X, Y, and Z may affect and change the operation of A, and so on.

Factors on the inside

To simplify matters considerably, we may take these in two groups:

Genetics and maturation

When a child is conceived, the male egg (sperm) releases twenty-three minute particles and these join twenty-three others from the female egg (ovum). These forty-six particles, called chromosomes, constitute all the chemical information which the father and mother pass on to their child. Along each chromosome, little snake-like formations, 'genes', are located, and these form essentially the basis of inheritance —heredity. As the baby grows, the cells of the body divide and multiply, and in every cell of the body the genes on the chromosomes exercise control over the growth and development processes (timing, rate, extent of growth, etc.).

Some genes (individually or collectively) are responsible for highly specific characteristics in an individual—e.g. hair and eye colour, skin pigment, some rare diseases, etc. Other genes (usually working polygenetically, that is in groups) are not responsible for any specific characteristic, but determine the trend and general nature of development. This is the way in which genes work for intelligence—in a general and non-specific way. As far as we know, we do not inherit genes which determine on their own characteristics such as musical ability, chess-playing skills, football skills or, indeed, intelligence. Genes do provide the basis of skills (if you like, one's various potentials for developing in certain ways), and genes do determine the level of skill beyond which you are not able to develop (although this issue is quite complicated). (See Callaway, 1970.) But all development must take place in a social environment, and therefore genes must have an environment in which to express their characteristics. In human development, it is the genetic factors operating in conjunction (or interacting) with the environmental factors which determine characteristics of abilities and skills. This is a very fundamental and important point.

To summarise—there is a genetic component in intelligence which is inherited from the parents. (An interesting model of the mechanisms of inheritance is given by Li, 1971.) But it is not specific, and it is not completely pre-programmed and beyond alteration. Hereditary factors probably set the upper limits in development, yet much depends on the factors operating in the environment in deciding (i) the direction of development, and (ii) the levels finally reached.

An individual matures as these genetic programmes unfold, as for example, with the onset of puberty and the course of bodily growth in general. So, maturation is under genetic control mostly. However, the environment is playing its part in interacting with these genetic programmes and environmental factors are able to exert some effect on maturation. (Note that the onset of puberty is getting earlier and earlier with each successive generation.) Once again, we have to acknowledge the complex web of interaction.

In the voluminous literature on intelligence support for the view that genetic factors are important in determining intelligence (a view that is not entirely rejected here, of course) comes from at least two areas of research: race and twin studies.

The 'race' evidence largely rests on observed differences between black (negro) and white children on IQ and attainment tests on average. The scores on these tests for groups of black children tend to

What affects intelligence?

be lower than for groups of white children (Eysenck, 1971). This can, of course, be explained in terms of inferior environment—IQ scores of black children are lower because of poorer circumstances. However, in 1969 Arthur Jensen reopened a long-standing controversy by challenging this environmental explanation. He argued that IQs were lower because of inferior genes which the black groups had inherited from their parents. Jensen's arguments are quite technical and we can only sketch the briefest of outlines here. First, he points out that many studies have shown that black children in the USA score, on average, about fifteen points lower on IQ tests than their white peers (a quite substantial difference). Then, second, he maintains that individual differences in IQ among any group of people are determined in part by genetic factors (which is a sensible and acceptable point to most). He is quite adamant, however, that these differences are 80 per cent determined by genetic differences (a point which is not sensible and acceptable to most). So, third, if IQs are inherited to this high degree within groups (and given the substantial differences found between groups—black and white) then these black–white differences are also due to genetic factors. Now, there are some very technical intricacies in these arguments and counter-arguments, one being the doubt about 80 per cent genetic determination, and another about the danger of extrapolating from talking about differences between groups to inferring differential causation between individuals. We would perhaps do the reader some injustice if we were to follow these intricacies now (see further reading). It is perhaps sufficient here to note three points.

1 Jensen argued that on the strength of these conclusions 'compensatory education has been tried and has apparently failed' and mostly because the young negro supposedly has a lower genetic potential to benefit from any compensatory help given. In chapter 1, Jensen's ideas on the nature of intelligence were discussed—Level I being held to be 'associative' ability common to all social classes, and Level II being 'cognitive' ability which is based on Level I, but not equally available to all. He sees the main implications of this line of reasoning to be that children of allegedly low genetic potential should have an educational curriculum based on Level I material (mechanical memory and rote learning) and those better endowed should have a more conceptually demanding type of education, in line with Level II ability (Jensen, 1970);

2 Many geneticists and psychologists would argue that we are at present quite unable to draw any firm conclusions as to the extent to

which genetic differences are responsible for IQ differences between groups (like black and white children) living and growing in different circumstances (Rose, 1972);

3 Other psychologists would argue that the supposed genetic effects can in fact be attributed to poorly understood environmental effects. Stinchcombe (1969), for example, emphasises that little is known about the complexities of the environment, in detailed terms, and talking of any proportional effects of heredity and environment is therefore of little value.

The 'twin' studies are again quite technical and only a brief sketch is presented here (see further reading). Many studies have reported that the more closely related two people are, the more chance there is that their IQ scores will be similar (Erlenmeyer-Kimling and Jarvik, 1963). For example, identical twins (supposedly possessing identical genes because they resulted from the splitting of one cell) have IQ scores which are highly correlated (usually very similar scores); fraternal twins (resulting from two cells) have IQ scores quite highly correlated; brothers and sisters of different ages have scores reasonably correlated; parent and child share fairly similar scores; child and stranger scores are hardly correlated at all. Thus, the more close the genetic bond, the more similar the IQ score. However, this argument can be turned around—people who are related tend to share the same environments, and the nearer they are in age, the more similar the environment. Thus, identical twins have very similar IQs because they are reared in the same environment. An objection to this counter argument is that if one examines the scores of twins who have been reared separately (in say two foster homes) they still have similar IQs, though again an examination of the two environments often shows similarity.

Furthermore, a disturbing controversy has been extensively discussed by Kamin (1974) and many others on the probably fraudulent nature of the main line of twin studies—those of Burt. Burt's major studies in this area (e.g. 1966) have been used extensively by people like Jensen in developing a genetic line of argument and in calculating 'heritability' coefficients. It now seems as if Burt did not report his findings in an accurate and scientifically respectable manner, and that much of his data was dishonestly manipulated and therefore highly suspect.

So the arguments take on more and more technical detail and become quite involved (see Brody and Brody, 1976). At this stage it is probably sufficient to note one major conclusion: we must recognise and state clearly that the idea that both genetic factors (as shown in race and twin studies) and environmental factors are crucial for the development of children's intellects and skills.

Other biological factors

In a sense, certain biological factors are both 'inside' and 'outside', and although not appertaining to intelligence in isolation, they have been shown to be of some importance in child development generally (Davie *et al.*, 1972).

Many pre- and peri-natal conditions (whilst the child is in the womb and around the period of birth) have been found to affect development in general and some specifically to lead to the lowering of intellectual functioning to subnormal levels. For instance, the age of the mother can be important. For mums less than twenty years old or over thirty-five, the rate of infant mortality is higher; and if children live they stand greater risks of being retarded. If all families were completed before mothers became thirty-eight, the incidence of mongolism would be severely reduced. (Clarke and Clarke, 1974).

The diet of the mother, especially in her last few months of pregnancy (and continuing for the child to around eighteen months) is also crucial. Some recent work has shown that the brain follows a spurt of growth in the three months before birth to about eighteen months or so after birth, and during this time some very crucial building work is going on in the central nervous system and brain. If this spurt is simply slowed down, it will do irreparable damage to the brain—and a poor diet will do just this. Once this growth spurt is over (that is, after a child is two years old) a deficiency in the diet will not greatly affect the potential of the brain, but up to two years the brain potential can be permanently reduced (Dobbing and Smart, 1974; Lewin, 1975).

There are other biological factors which run a serious risk of affecting development—smoking, drinking and drug taking in pregnancy, disease during pregnancy (e.g. rubella, or german measles), abnormal delivery, length of pregnancy, and so on. The main point to grasp here is that all these so-called biological factors are operating together with environmental or social factors (and this means that research findings are usually quite complicated to interpret) and this leads us to the factors operating in the environment—or on the outside.

Factors on the outside

It is impossible to divide these factors into meaningful categories as separate entities because, apart from the other considerations, life just does not work in such a simplistic fashion! The arbitrary divisions are made only for convenience of presentation—we look at factors one at a time to keep the thing down to manageable proportions, but it should be emphasised that in reality sub-divisions overlap and interlock with one another.

The manner in which these factors work is very problematical. We are very much in a state of description—that is, painting pictures of how things look and saying that X is related to Y, etc. Some factors are very wide and probably operate in very gross, macro fashion. Other factors may be much more subtle, if just as powerful. One can take a photograph of poor housing conditions, but how can a person's attitude to another be represented? We are a long way off causes and mechanisms—we are not yet able to say exactly why this factor has this effect and stipulate precisely the manner in which it operates.

Incidentally, it is interesting to ponder upon the fact that much of what follows has only been appreciated as being of some importance and significance in recent times—it is easy to think that it is all just common sense, but as de Mause (1974) has cogently pointed out, our concepts about childhood and what affects development (and intelligence) have changed drastically over the centuries, and are still in a process of reformulation.

Social class and cultural factors

Many aspects of human life seem to be related to social class (as defined by the Registrar General's classification system based on the occupation of the father: highest being social class I and lowest social class V). Generally, social class V (unskilled manual workers) children perform less well on measures of basic school subjects and skills such as reading, number, spelling, ability, creativity, adjustment, etc. These differences are often quite substantial, and increase as the children get older (Davie, Butler and Goldstein, 1972; Wedge and Prosser, 1973; Fogelman and Goldstein, 1976). We must be careful not to allow social class to become an explanation for the differences found—that is, to say that poor reading levels are such because of social class V—but it can provide some useful clues as to the origins of the differences found. As for intelligence, we can say that there are significant differences in measured intelligence (IQ) between the social classes. (But within each class there is the whole range of IQ).

Evidence has been accumulating that certain social class background factors are frequently associated with below average intellectual functioning. This has often been explained in terms of social disadvantage with an associated deprived environment—so psychologically the children involved are not sufficiently stimulated with the optimal amount and variety of proper experiences (Uzgiris, 1970). This debate in itself is complex and has been extensively debated (see, e.g. Cole and Bruner, 1971; Rutter and Madge, 1976), and many would argue that this idea of psychological 'deficit' is not as clear cut as would seem (Labov, 1969; Ginsburg, 1972). Instead, we are in the description versus mechanisms problem again, and the way in which these social factors operate on cognitive development is still largely unknown. Research is required into more specific aspects for progress here to be achieved (Clarke and Clarke, 1974).

Swift (1968) points out that we must examine these issues in the context of other cultural aspects—social class is only one very broad category of the total cultural conditions of the community. Therefore, if we look at various communities (e.g. rural and urban) differences in IQs between one community and another are often noticeable. This illustrates some effects of the environment. Often the implication is that some form of regional deprivation, or difference, has a direct effect on children's thinking skills. Some very famous studies have illustrated this: Gordon (1923) examined the IQs of both canal boat and gypsy families in the UK and found that as the children became older the IQ levels decreased—a well-known result in subnormality research known as 'progressive mental retardation'. Sherman and Key (1932) and Wheeler (1942) working in the USA looked at isolated mountain communities and found that IQs were well below the national norms, and again decreased with age. More recently, Lesser, Fifer and Clark (1965) looked at four groups of children in New York: the ethnic communities were Chinese, Jewish, Negro and Puerto Rican (six–seven years old). Rather than comparing IQs, these researchers looked at the differences in *patterns* of ability (verbal, reasoning, number, space). Previous studies which looked at cultural influences found that language skills are particularly susceptible to the kind of culture being experienced. Lesser *et al.* found considerable variations in the patterns they found between the ethnic groups, and that although the middle-class children scored higher on each test, these different patterns of ability were stable irrespective of the particular social class. That is, each group had a different pattern (low verbal, high space *v.* high verbal, low space for example) and within each group the middle-class children tended to have similar patterns only higher scores all round. This amply demonstrates the effect which the culture can exercise on the mental abilities of children.

Another approach is to look closely at one community, and Wiseman did this in his 1964 survey of an area in Manchester. He found that certain conditions *within* the community were related to IQ (though this does not necessarily imply any 'causes')—for instance, persons per acre, infectious diseases, infant mortality, housing conditions, family sizes. On a slightly different note, Morris (1966) surveyed reading ability in Kent and found a relationship between environmental handicap and reading difficulty. These studies serve to remind us that the conditions within a certain community are able to affect measures of ability and attainment. (For a general discussion of cultural influence, see Serpell 1976.)

It is clear that children from communities with poor cultural conditions and those from low social class backgrounds are, on average, lower in 'effective intelligence' and Vernon (1969) postulates three reasons: (i) there are certainly some genetic differences between classes; (ii) they have usually received poor pre- and post-natal care; (iii) their parents have not brought them up to be as intelligent or as motivated in intellectual achievement. And this takes us to the next factor.

Family and home background

If we look at the performance of children at around fifteen to eighteen months little differences are found between social classes. But by three years there are some substantial differences (Hindley, 1965) and these increase as the children grow older, as shown by the National Child Development Study (Davie, Butler and Goldstein, 1972). Some researchers (e.g. Hess and Shipman, 1965) would argue that this is the result of the differences in how mothers handle their children. Indeed, mothers appear to be quite central, and this is not stating the obvious—surveys have shown that low maternal IQ is the best predictor of a low functioning child who may need special schooling (Heber and Garber, 1971). Thus, if we wished to predict which babies were eventually to need special schooling, our best bet would be to take the children of low IQ mothers.

Why might this be so? It has been shown by many researchers (e.g.

Fraser, 1959) that the middle-class mother is more often involved in talking directly to her child, structuring and elaborating the environment and giving verbal encouragement and praise. The family in general, and the mother in particular need, then, to provide a *varied* amount of stimulation, to allow exploration, play and varieties of perceptual experience. Children ought to have the opportunity to engage in 'thought-provoking' activities and discussion, with the use of books and suitable periodicals, and involving as much as possible a significant adult. In rearing the child, the 'climate' seems important— democratic but demanding, a home which encourages resourcefulness and independence. These probably lead to clearer and richer concepts, not to mention a strong belief in one's 'self'. This all strengthens the ability 'to cope' (Vernon, 1969). We also know that there is a relation between IQ and family size— the more children in a family, the greater the probability of lower IQs—which might well indicate that adult attention is important in the development of intelligence, so that with more children adult attention for each decreases (Nisbet and Entwistle, 1967).

There is quite a substantial amount of research which tells us, one way or another, that certain factors operate in a rather subtle, yet quite powerful way in influencing the intelligence of children.

Some large studies, following up thousands of children over many years, show that parental interest and encouragement can be important factors in part in determining ability and attainment scores. In certain cases these factors of interest and encouragement shown by parents towards their children's school work are more powerful than some of the other factors discussed above (Douglas, 1964; Douglas, Ross and Simpson, 1968). There is also a strong association between parental educational level and the ability and attainments of their children, obviously a connected finding (Davie, Butler and Goldstein, 1972).

Kagan (1970) argues forcefully that a subtle influence within the home is that of the mother's sense of effectiveness and levels of expectancy. The lower-social-class mother is more than likely quite ignorant of how children develop. She is likely to believe that she has no real effect on what sort of child she has (his behaviour, personality, intelligence, etc.) and as such is likely to have a low expectation of her child's capabilities. Thus, she is not likely to stretch her child, or seek help, or visit the school, and in general will accept her lot and feel a lack of control. Moreover, these attitudes are very likely to be transmitted to her children, and they too may inherit poor levels of motivation and expectancies of failure.

Another area of evidence which suggests the subtle influence within the home on ability is that referred to as the 'first born phenomenon'. We have already mentioned that children's IQ scores decrease as the size of family increases. Another oft-quoted and related finding is that the eldest child tends to do much better than later-born children in general (and regardless of ability) and also has higher IQ scores, (Douglas, Ross and Simpson, 1968; Davie *et al.*, 1972). Thus, if you are a member of a small family your IQ is likely to be higher than if you are one of a large family; and also if you are the eldest you are likely to have a higher IQ than your brothers and sisters, and whether you have or have not, you are still likely to read more books, join more clubs, be more popular, do better at school, go further in higher education, and so on. Why? It has been suggested that children in such positions receive more attention from adults and also are given the chance to teach younger brothers and sisters, and these experiences result in higher IQ scores and a faster rate of intellectual development (Zajonc, 1975).

Schooling

Though probably not as important a factor as the others listed, we can still say that attending school has some effect on the IQs of children. Some would argue that important aspects of intelligent behaviour are learned outside school (mainly before schooling begins). But Vernon (1969) stresses that the sheer amount of schooling, regardless of quality, helps to promote the kind of reasoning measured in IQ tests. We often hear the call for pre-school education and there are many reasons for this. But for our purpose we can be reasonably sure that if early school experience (of the sort which makes suitable demands upon a child's thinking) can stretch the cognitive skills of children then intellectual powers will be strengthened. Later in the book we mention Hunt's 'problem of the match', a topic which involves stretching a child's thinking powers.

Pidgeon (1970) has demonstrated that children's intelligence scores (and more important, possibly, their attainment scores) can be affected quite dramatically by subtle factors operating within the school. He argues that the beliefs held by teachers about the concepts and nature of intelligence determine to no small extent the levels of achievement expected of pupils. Indeed, one reason for writing this book was to help teachers form a clear and more accurate view of how present day psychologists view intelligence—if teachers get hold of the wrong end of this particular stick they can do great harm to their pupils. If they are well versed in modern conceptions and interpretations then they are able to alter pupils' functioning quite considerably.

One study which purported to show great effects of teacher expectations on pupil performance was by Rosenthal and Jacobson (1968). There are serious technical faults in this study and thus we need to be very careful when looking at the reported results. Teachers were told that on the basis of psychological tests, certain pupils would make 'intellectual spurts'. In fact, these pupils were chosen at random. But they eventually made significant IQ gains compared with the IQs of their classmates. Despite the serious technical faults in this study, many would accept the validity of the principle behind the findings (Williams, 1976). This principle is known as the 'self-fulfilling prophecy' and it has at least one implication for school organisation. In short, the argument says that we are not able to measure the potential ability of children, IQ scores being no more than fairly accurate indicators of present levels. Thus any decision made to stream children into A, B, C, D, and E classes, grades or groups will be somewhat misguided. If children do respond over their school life as A or B and so on, then this could be due to at least two reasons: either that they were in fact A, B, etc. children, or that low or high expectancies led to a self-fulfilling prophecy and they responded in ways expected of them. Indeed children are very flexible and quite adept in behaving in ways that fit adult expectations. IQ figures for children are able to change quite dramatically over a period of years (see the following sections in this chapter). The subtle influences operating within a school are able either to help children develop or effectively to slow down their development.

Cognitive factors

Implied in much of the above discussion are the various effects which factors can exert on a person's motivation and attitude towards life, and more directly the ways in which home and school can increase or depress these 'personality' types of considerations. If being intelligent is about coping with the world and developing a sense of personal effectiveness, then clearly the links here are important. But can we be more specific about just what the home and school can do in helping a child to be more intelligent? Can we say just how we can teach a child, or more correctly enhance his learning, with respect to these 'coping' skills? Many would argue that early in development, the best way to achieve this is to ensure that the motor, perceptual and linguistic experience that a child has are at the correct level in terms of variety and the level of demand made upon the developing thinking skills, (e.g. Vernon, 1969; Hess and Shipman, 1965). Why should this be so? One possible mechanism here is that of learning transfer—a 'good' home will engineer many similar situations in which a child can apply a particular skill. He may extend his understanding of that skill by learning how he can use it in a variety of situations—he can transfer his learning to other related areas.

We have referred to linguistic skills previously in this chapter and certainly the place of language in the course of development (and thus its place in intelligence) is a crucial and yet debatable issue. When a child is forming conceptions of the world language normally plays a large part, and therefore is definitely implicated in some way in the development of intelligence. As noted previously, one debate at the moment in the social sciences is whether certain 'disadvantaged' children are deprived linguistically, or whether they are using a different linguistic system. This leads to two interpretations which involve the place of language in measures of intelligence. Thus, low IQ can be regarded as either (a) realistic because the child has poor language skills due to his linguistic deprivation and thus unable to do the tests well; or (b) unrealistic because the test is culturally highly biased and as such a child's linguistic skills are just so different from those required to answer the test questions and so render the test quite inappropriate.

It seems highly probable that the processes which lie beneath a child's language are related (though not necessarily the same) to those processes behind his thinking, and these issues which are obviously central in any discussion of intelligence are developed in chapter 4.

Attempts to raise IQ

There is a large body of literature which discusses attempts to increase the IQs (and, consequently, the intellectual powers) of children (see Rutter and Madge, 1976). These experiments have usually been concerned either with preventing babies and infants developing into dull children and adults, or at later points in time intervening in the lives of already fairly dull children in an attempt to raise their thinking powers. There is only space here to provide a flavour of the types of work reported.

One fascinating and extremely important study in prevention and early intervention is that of the 'Milwaukee Project' (Garber and Heber, 1977). Surveys of a particularly poor area of Milwaukee (in terms of extreme overcrowding, poor living conditions, and low educational level) showed that it gave rise to a very high proportion of children who were educationally subnormal (mild mental retardation). Further work showed that by far the highest predictor of subnormality within this particular area was maternal IQ—children whose mothers have an IQ of 80 or below are likely to be at very high risk for mental retardation. On the basis of these findings, forty women with newborn children were selected who had WAIS Full Scale IQs of 75 or less and who already had children. These forty babies, all highly likely to grow up as mentally retarded, were randomly allocated to either an experimental or control group (twenty in each). The experimental group, with full co-operation of the families, were started upon a two-pronged programme. First, an infant stimulation programme was started where the babies received intensive treatment, for seven hours a day, five days a week, with properly trained teachers. The curriculum concentrated on language and problem-solving skills for the appropriate age (it started from three to six months of age to six years), thus having a cognitive-language orientation within a structured environment—teaching was very prescriptive with clearly laid out objectives. The emotional needs of the children were not forgotten, however, and the investigators laid much stress on securing the highest motivational attitudes in the children (Heber, 1971; Heber and Garber, 1971). Second, a maternal rehabilitation programme ensured intensive work with both the mothers (and some fathers) and the children. The programme gave help and training in basic 'three Rs', home economics, child care, and some vocational training.

The results of this prospective study will not be fully known till the children get well into adolescence. However, regular evaluation of both groups (the control group, of course, having no programme except the normal welfare and education services) show some very fascinating initial comparisons. Although various types of measures were made (language tests, experimental problem-solving tasks and so on) the general indication over the first eight or nine years is that the experimental group is considerably more advanced intellectually (and to an extent socially) than the control—the mean IQ (WISC) at around a hundred months (eight years) of the experimental group was thirty points higher than the control (110 v 80)—a massive difference. Although this study is not yet finished, and given the cautions noted by Garber and Heber, they do conclude that 'early intervention into the lives of seriously disadvantaged families at risk for retardation with a direct, intensive, and comprehensive rehabilitation effort can effectively prevent retardation' (1977).

Other studies have attempted to intervene at later points in order to boost intellectual functioning, the earliest probably being the work of Skeels and Dye (1939). The most famous series, however, are known collectively as the 'Headstart' compensatory education programme in the USA dating from the 1960s and still continuing (for a review, see Bronfenbrenner 1975). On the whole, most of these apparently failed to show any effects at all, or any effects shown faded when the programmes finished. Such programmes, usually a few weeks during the summer vacation with pre-school children from slum areas, often poorly structured, were hardly likely to have had any great effect unless intensively prolonged for considerable periods. A few well-thought-out and executed programmes were successful (e.g. Gray and Klaus, 1965, 1970), and there is some evidence that early programmes did benefit the children who are now adolescent (Lewin, 1977). 'Headstart' has changed in design since the earlier days—the projects now concentrate on one-year programmes, and more emphasis is given to under-threes, their parents and home-visiting schemes. One emphasis is to work towards involving parents more in the educational process, and encouraging them to feel more effective as agents in the development of their children. For a review of British projects, see Rutter and Madge (1976), and Pilling and Pringle (1978).

Evidence of increased IQ scores resulting from changed environmental circumstances comes from other sources. Studies reported, known as 'isolated cases', have shown dramatic increases in intellectual functioning following severe adversity (Davis, 1947; Koluchova, 1972, 1976). Typically, children have been cruelly isolated in cellars or attics for years, and when found were mentally retarded, often severely so. After treatment, IQ levels have reached the normal range. Several investigators have shown that children transferred to good foster homes (from poor institutions) have improved their IQs. Skodak and Skeels (1949) followed the progress of sixteen children of defective mothers who had been placed in foster homes before they were six months old. The average IQ of a foster child was around 100, much higher than their real mother's score, the differences due in part to the effect of the foster-home environment.

All these lines of evidence, admittedly from children in special circumstances of one kind or another, do point to the various ways in which both inside and outside factors can operate over many years in affecting measured intelligence. We return to one or two of these studies in chapter 5 when we examine what sort of situation stimulates intellectual growth. But before this we draw the evidence together in a major theoretical formulation.

Complex and continuous interactions

So what affects intelligence? Some psychologists think that differences in ability are the result of differences in environmental demands (Ferguson, 1954). Others, like Jensen, would argue that the environment works according to some rule of a threshold—that over a certain level of stimulation it ceases to have an effect and differences between people are then due to genetic differences in the main.

It would seem, however, that there is little sense in pursuing this line of controversy since it is quite clear to many psychologists (having possibly a firm practical orientation) that it is the complex and continuous interactions of the various factors discussed that determine effective intelligence. Clarke and Clarke (1974) say that 'human development is mediated by slow, unfolding, cumulative and powerful biological and psycho-social interactions'. Their comment serves to underline Hebb's (1949) comment that intelligence is developed by a completely necessary innate potential, interacting with a completely necessary environment, and that these interact in a complex way over many years of development.

The complexity of this does need to be emphasised. Some hold that it is just a simple way out of the argument, and that everyone is in agreement that both hereditary and environmental factors are important (Rosenthal, 1968). However, as Erlenmeyer-Kimling (1977) is at pains to point out, gene-environment interactions are exceedingly complex in the various ways in which they operate, are immensely difficult to research and study and are by no means accepted by all. As Hebb has pointed out, the area of a field is determined by the length and breadth, the two dimensions being inextricably involved in the area calculation. It would make no sense to ask 'Which is the most important in determining the area?' Surely, then, it is the function of education to manipulate these factors in order to improve the development of intelligence in children, and this would be a much more fruitful line of debate than a purely theoretical one of proportions allocated to biological, social factors and the like.

Sameroff and Chandler (1975) go even one stage further and argue in terms of a transactional model, rather than in interactionist terms. For them, an interaction model is inadequate because the 'inside' and 'outside' factors are not constant over time—at each moment of the day, important characteristics of the child and his environment change, and these changes influence each other. 'The child alters his environment and in turn is altered by the changed world he has created' (Sameroff and Chandler, 1975). Thus a more dynamic theory of transaction is required to account for these changing circumstances, and which stresses the plastic nature of the environment and also the way the person is active in his own development. A child does not simply react to the world in a passive way. Rather, he actively works upon it, organises it and provides some structure to his experiences—he is in a perpetual state of active re-organisation. This transactional model is very much in line with the cognitive view of development outlined in chapter 4, and with certain views on personality (Mischel, 1968) and it has immense educational implications (see chapters 4 and 5).

If we briefly pursue some implications of these interactional/ transactional models, then the practical consequences might become rather clearer. These models lead us to at least two major themes—the importance of early experience in cognitive development, and the constancy of an individual's IQ over development. Both issues are very large, and the purpose here is to do no more than identify important links with the general content of this chapter (see Clarke and Clarke, 1976b, 1978). It would seem to follow that if intelligent behaviour is largely determined by the complex and continuing interactions and transactions of the genes and environmental experiences, then the effects of the first five years or so will not be as critical as many have thought. Indeed, it is important to ensure optimal growing and learning conditions during these early years, but development does not end at age five, and there are many instances where children have 'caught-up' later (Feuerstein, 1971; Kagan, 1976). Let us be very clear about this implication—it is important to design and carry out early screening procedures, for example, to identify children at risk and, generally, to provide the best support and educational environment in order to ensure optimal learning and development. However, if we think that these early years are so critical that nothing much can be done to help children once they are out of the 'critical period', then we are very wrong in our assumptions. As we have seen, attempts to improve IQ are possible, and though many have strong reservations (Vernon, 1976a) there is plenty of evidence to show that IQs are not fixed early in life, and many children's IQs do move up and down quite considerably as they get older—there is an almost total lack of correlation of IQ scores obtained in infancy and adulthood on the same subjects (e.g. McCall *et al.*, 1973; Clarke and Clarke, 1972, 1976a).

In other words, we should not be over-pessimistic (or optimistic) in thinking that a child's intellectual level is necessarily fixed and permanent for all time from birth and the early years onwards. There are large problems in trying to predict just how development will take place in people (Clarke, 1978), and unless children are physically damaged in some way (e.g. some form of brain damage) we should not be too quick off the mark in making unjustifiable assumptions, decisions and actions. We should be concerned to develop the native ability in children as much as is possible, and we can state firmly that very few, if any, children are intellectually as developed as their innate inheritance would allow (Donaldson, 1978). So, it is the job of parents, teachers, psychologists, etc., to utilise whatever leads and information are available in improving the rate of development. The remaining chapters, hopefully, continue to provide pointers in this highly important goal.

Conclusion and implications

1 The topic of what factors affect intelligence is exceedingly complex, and there are certainly no easy answers.

2 Both inside and outside factors are crucial for the development of intellctual skills, and both are interacting. Thus, there seems little point in deciding the exact contribution of each factor since the picture is very much one of intricately interwoven patterns.

3 Inheritance of intelligence is not a straightforward matter. We do not have 'genes for intelligence'. Genes provide the basis for and possibly the ceiling of cognitive skills. But, they must have an environment in which to express themselves—development must take place in a social environment. So it is the genetic factors operating in conjunction with the environmental ones which determine characteristics of abilities and skills (and this has obvious implications for parents and teachers).

4 The more obvious implications for parents and teachers, work-

ing within the framework of the chapter headings, are as follows:

(i) for the factors operating on the inside, we can state that intelligence is not fixed by the genes in some pre-programmed and pre-determined manner; thus, IQ is able to be raised within broad genetic limits. Various other biological factors help to determine brain potential, especially during the period of brain growth spurt; often, in many instances, something can be done to reduce risk of damage and permanent deficit.

(ii) for the factors operating on the outside, we can broadly and generally state that certain aspects of the environment are involved in developing intelligence; if those who have suffered severe deprivation are moved to an enriched setting, there are good chances of improving their IQ scores; scores are affected by the cultural conditions of the community, and in particular there are strong associations with social class; the home background (especially the mother) and schooling experienced by the child can affect his development, and in particular the language skills seem profoundly important in these respects. Also important are encouragement, interest and above all attitudes towards the developing child which are adopted by parents and teachers.

5 On a more general note, we can state that the myth of measuring innate ability still persists. We cannot measure biological potential. The measures of intelligence that we have (IQ) are widely based achievement scores indicating present capacity, and they perhaps predict the future with some accuracy because they sample more general conceptual and reasoning skills which have been built up through experience. This implies that just as one is able to improve a child's score on a reading test (by improving his reading skills) then so one is able to improve IQ scores by improving his reasoning skills, language skills, etc. The scores as they stand are not final judgments. So, teaching should not be hampered or restricted by IQ results (he's no good at X because he is not too bright) but should be guided by the results of tests so that, starting from present levels, the teacher can devise programmes to increase the efficiency and development of thinking powers. This is a tall order, but it is possible, and the earlier one starts the better. These points are pursued further in the following chapters.

Chapter 4

The development of intelligence

Growth in understanding and knowing about the world is often referred to as 'intellectual' or 'cognitive' development. There have been many attempts to describe and explain the ways in which children's reasoning and thinking skills and abilities develop—the development of cognition. These attempts have often started off from different perspectives and premises, and made very different assumptions—for example, about how to investigate human behaviour. A particular instance is the conventional psychometric approach which was discussed in chapter 1. This test-based approach has been very concerned with investigating how hundreds of people perform on certain mental tests, and using sophisticated statistical procedures have described group trends which tell us little about actual individuals. This approach relies heavily on quantitative 'amounts'—the numbers called IQ scores—and describes intellectual development by drawing growth curves of scores. The behaviourist approach, by comparison, is very concerned with the stimulus situation and how altering this will affect responses and learning outcomes (see chapter 5). The developmental psychologist, being different again, is very concerned with finding landmarks and stages through which children pass in order to attain a particular level of thinking. This approach relies less on numbers and more on kinds or quantities of ability. When thinking about intellectual development, the psychometricians (using for example the MA) would tend to describe this in *continuous* terms—adding up the questions successfully answered, and the more a child scores correctly the more intellectually capable he is thought to be. The developmental psychologists, however, would think in terms of *discontinuities* of development—intellectual capability is not attained by simply getting better but by essentially changing ways of operating. It is hardly surprising then that one approach makes different and often diametrically opposed points from another. Some writers, for example Elkind (1971), Bolton (1972) and Guilford (1967), have tried to bring the quantitative and qualitative camps together and with some success.

In this chapter we focus initially upon the work of some developmental psychologists and consider how they view the growth of intelligence and abilities. We do this by looking first at the 'food for thought'—the units of thinking that the brain probably operates with—then at some developmental theories which try to explain how the 'machine' operates over the early years of development. An alternative 'process' approach is then examined, which leads us to look at the place of language in intellectual growth, and consequently on to a simple skills model that might have some educational usefulness. Finally, some conclusions and implications are drawn.

Before proceeding, let us be sure of the ideal, ultimate goal. We considered in chapter 2 various tests of intelligence and in chapter 3 certain factors which have been shown to be central in affecting scores on IQ tests (or which are strongly associated with IQs). This was all largely descriptive. What we need to know is much more about mechanisms which appertain to individual development. We need to know, as teachers, the 'whys' and 'hows' of individual development. Not merely what tends to be associated with what, but more what causes certain trends in individual behaviour. Take as an example one of the item types which appear in many standardised tests of intelligence. A child may be asked how two objects are alike—say a chair and a table. Now there are many answers to this indicating various levels of response—they are both toys in a doll's house, they are both made of wood, they are both pieces of furniture, they both are members of a set called 'dining suite', they both exhibit similar features of shape, texture, colour, etc. So behind this one seemingly simple question lies a hierarchy of response levels—from physical characteristics to functional and higher order abstract concepts.

This chapter is essentially about ways of getting behind this wrong/right score to the methods which children adopt in finding an answer. The objective here (and in chapter 5) is to go from description to explanation. With such information we can start to make the educational situation more effective, and improve the efficiency of children's brains and their learning. If we are to do things with children, from birth, which enhances their intellectual development, then we must move from 'common sense' (whatever that may be) and intuitive teaching to a more thought out system based upon how we

70 *The development of intelligence*

suppose a child's mind works. If we cannot get this right, then teaching will not be effective. Most children develop and learn almost despite their parents and teachers—their curious minds pick up and process information often despite the way it is presented. But is this good enough? Are these children developing and learning as efficiently as they might if we could clear away many stumbling blocks—in the teaching of reading and mathematics, for example? And what about children who have difficulties in learning and developing—the mentally handicapped, the children with specific learning difficulties and special educational needs (see Warnock, 1978). It is here where our common (intuitive) sense often fails us badly.

So it is very important to seek a theory of development which is acceptable. However, we are some way off this goal, and as Clarke has persistently pointed out over the years (e.g. Clarke, 1978), predicting human behaviour is a very problematic business, and developmental psychologists tend to devise models without acknowledging this difficulty.

The units of intellectual development

Before finding out about the ways in which we learn to understand and reason, we will consider the 'brain fodder' or cognitive units which provide the material content of thinking. What do we think with when we face the many small (and major) problems and decisions throughout every day of our lives?

Many important psychologists have referred to four or so broad units of intellectual activity, but unfortunately they have not always used the same words to indicate precisely the same meanings or intentions (e.g. Piaget, 1950; Bartlett, 1932; Hebb, 1949; Kagan and Lang, 1978; Bruner *et al.*, 1966; Mussen *et al.*, 1974; Neisser, 1967 and 1976). However, we can suggest four broad units as follows: (1) schemas, or schemata; (2) images; (3) symbols; and (4) concepts and rules. These units are often referred to as cognitive structures.

1 A schema (in the plural schemas or schemata) is the most basic unit, and refers to either a sequence of physical or mental action, or to a mental representation of an event. Schemas are very basic ways of organising and classifying experience, and are not necessarily related to mental 'pictures' or images nor to language. A schema such as the arm shaking action of a baby may be the most basic way of representing an event—in this case this co-ordinated sequence of action repre-

sents a shaking rattle. What is the most distinctive (or most important) element or feature of an experience or event? Answer this, and you are representing that event in the most fundamental way, probably. Another way of referring to this is by talking about 'plans' which people adopt in order to direct their actions. Miller, Galanter and Pribram (1960) refer to a 'plan' which controls 'the order in which a sequence of operations is to be performed'. Intelligence can be thought of as a cumulative building up of such schemas, which become more complex and adaptable with experience (see Woodward, 1971 for a developmental discussion of this idea).

2 An image, or mental picture, is an elaboration of the basic skeleton of the schema. It is a more detailed, elaborate and conscious representation built upon the schema. In a way it would be similar to a snap-shot photograph, and a particular gift in recalling such images is called 'eidetic' imagery.

3 Symbols differ from schemas and images in that they are more arbitrary, abstract representations. A child can express meaning in a way that comes to stand for something else. Red stands for danger, a stick can be a sword, or gun or wand! The squiggles now being read are symbolic, as is the system of sounds called language. Symbols, which generally represent one specific event, are part of the fourth cognitive unit, the concept.

4 Concepts stand for the common aspects in a group of objects or events. In a group of schemas or symbols, certain similarities and differences may be extracted, and a concept might be developed which represents some common feature. For example, Mussen, Conger and Kagan (1974) refer to simple pencil drawings by children of a house. A seven-year-old represents the drawing as a schema, that is fairly stereotyped sequences of action with a central door and four corner windows. A three-year-old would scribble some lines and this symbol would be called 'a house'. An adult would regard the picture as potentially representing many sorts of houses from terraced to detached four-bedroomed, and probably transfer to the picture a set of complex relations about the living conditions of mankind. The adult is working with a fully developed concept of 'houses'. A further category is often added—that of rules which are formulated to connect concepts together in, say, solving problems (these may be formal rules called algorithms, or rules of thumbs called heuristics—see Farnham-Diggory, 1972). Let us pose the question 'Why schemas to concepts?' Generally, it would seem that even from birth an infant is very actively involved in seeking out regularities in the world (Bower, 1977). The

urge seems to be concerned with efficient organisation of the world to enhance understanding of it. Put another way, information has to be processed, and because there is such a wealth and density of sensory material, some strategy is developed to cope.

The formation of concepts is central to this strategy—that is, in the development of functions which enable the child to process information. The child has to discriminate features of the world and to abstract common elements. This allows the otherwise overwhelming complexity of information to be handled efficiently. Development of concepts provides a sort of intellectual shorthand allowing the learner to store information and reflect upon experience more economically. Using concepts, then, reduces complexity and also the cognitive load or demand which the learner has to utilise. As we noted repeatedly in chapter 3, cultural influences have a large effect on this process of growth, as these experiences interact with the genetically controlled maturational process. This is often taken to mean that the intelligence of a child should be seen as a set of developing cognitive skills—and certain of these skills have often been called various names by various developmental psychologists.

Developmental approaches

The formation of concepts in the study of intelligence has been studied by some developmental psychologists and their ideas have exerted powerful effects on curriculum design and teaching methods. We look at two major thinkers below—Piaget and Bruner—but first we consider a generalised sketch which sets the scene for these accounts.

A general sketch

This sketch of a general model is intended as only a highly simplified introduction to the particular theories advanced by people such as Piaget and Bruner. Other writers have referred to similar sketches, such as Johnson and Myklebust (1967), Gagné (1977) (see chapter 5), Neisser (1976), Ausubel (1968), Schmidt (1973) and Lunzer (1970)—though these are not necessarily all developmental psychologists.

As indicated above in looking at the units of intellectual activity, it is apparent that children must learn to discriminate the important features of an object or situation before they can group together the common elements—before classifications are made, similarities and differences must be perceived. After classifications have been formed —e.g. all round objects—then concepts are developed, used and modified in order to understand how the world works. From concrete concepts, some people form higher-order abstract concepts, connected by logical rules. Diagrammatically, this is shown in figure 4.1.

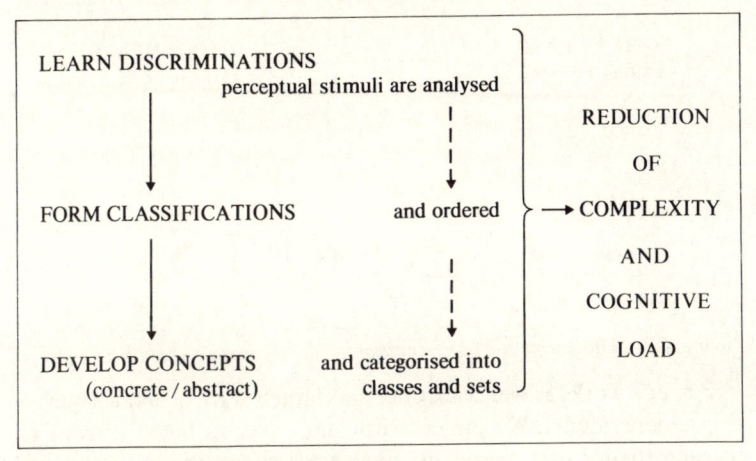

```
LEARN DISCRIMINATIONS
            perceptual stimuli are analysed
      |                                          REDUCTION
      |              |
      |              |                              OF
      ↓              ↓
FORM CLASSIFICATIONS    and ordered          → COMPLEXITY

      |                                           AND
      |              |
      |              |                          COGNITIVE
      ↓              ↓
DEVELOP CONCEPTS    and categorised into        LOAD
  (concrete / abstract)   classes and sets
```

Figure 4.1   The formation of concepts

The general line of theory has taken this a little further. It would seem that early in life the child is operating on his world in a largely perceptual manner—doing things with his body and generally involving all his senses in his activities. He is not, as such, thinking. This type of activity has been called sensori-motor 'thinking'. Later in life the child has not as much need to be so actively engaged, and can find out by operating conceptually—by applying a developing logical, conceptual system to the world—he can think and reason without necessarily having actually to do anything. In an important way, then, we have a series of quite different methods of knowing and understanding. This is summarised in figure 4.2.

A number of points need to be made with regard to this tentative general model: (1) the nature of the world in terms of 'reality' is essentially an individual act of construction and we have to build this 'phenomenological' knowledge up for ourselves; (2) this process of constructing reality in our heads is not only a matter of maturation and growing biologically bigger—the child is actively involved in his own development (at first very practically so) and the cultural

74 *The development of intelligence*

experience in which he partakes interact substantively with his biological capacity (this is one reason why exploratory behaviour, play and the encouragement of curiosity are such important aspects of early childhood); (3) all the 'edges', at least, are blurred—development can never be a clear cut, all or nothing business; (4) the place of language in this cognitive system is central.

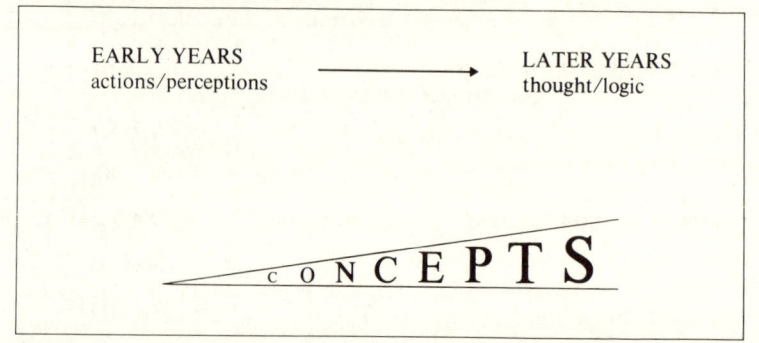

```
        EARLY YEARS                              LATER YEARS
        actions/perceptions      ———▶            thought/logic




                              C O N C E P T S
```

Figure 4.2 Diagrammatic representation of developing conceptual thought

Piaget's work, as well as Bruner's, is largely a particular account of this general model. We can be a little more specific before moving on to each theory in more detail. Figure 4.3 shows the general model again, with the associated 'key words' from the theorist's work. It should be regarded as adequate only for introductory purposes, because the actual theories are extremely complicated affairs.

	SENSORI-MOTOR ↕ ↘ LANGUAGE ⟶ CONCEPTS ↗ PERCEPTION
PIAGET	ACTIONS ⟶ PRE-OPERATIONS ⟶ OPERATIONS sensori-motor ⟶ pre-conceptual ⟶ intuitive ⟶ concrete operations

BRUNER	ENACTIVE ————————————————▶
	   I C O N I C ————————▶
	      S Y M B O L I C

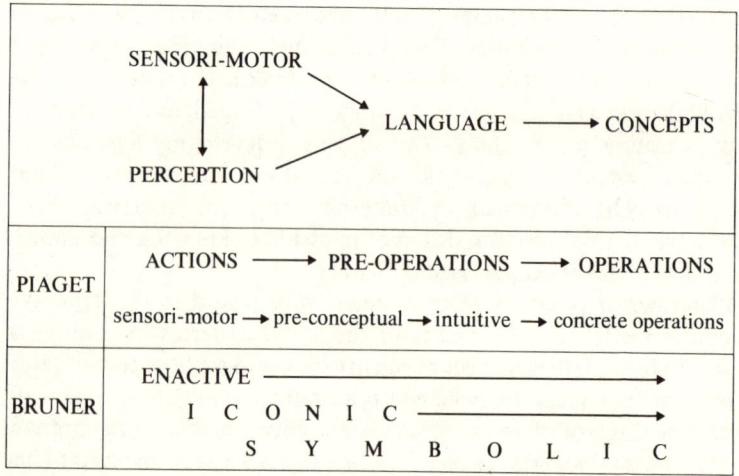

Figure 4.3 Diagrammatic summary of developmental stages and modes

Piaget's model

Jean Piaget's account of cognitive development is of mammoth proportions and is now creaking under the weight of some quite heavy criticism. It has been and still is, however, enormously important in many respects and will probably remain so for a good many years to come (see Bolton, 1972; Varma and Williams, 1976). All we can do here is briefly to describe his main ideas and educational implications, and present an outline of raised objections.

Piaget's background both as a student of biology and as a research assistant to Alfred Binet gave him his particular line of attack in studying children's minds (mainly his own children). He sees intelligence as the way an individual adapts to the environment, and although emphasis is given to experience in contributing to development, he argues that this is firmly based biologically in the maturational processes which are 'programmed' into the brain. Thus, he thinks that we all have the same intellectual path to follow, and this path takes us through a progressive series of cognitive structures or systems which lead to a series of stages of development: sensori-motor, preoperational and operational thinking.

On what sorts of activity are these stages based? Piaget postulates two sorts—actions and operations. An action carried out by the hand or eye (and so on) is the basic way of finding out what the world is like —you have to touch, push, feel, smell, see, etc. using all the senses and responding with movements (hence sensori-motor actions). A sequence of co-ordinated actions, to Piaget, is a schema and the elaboration of these schemas are the bases of intellectual development. The whole thing, then, is rooted in the actions performed.

As an older child or adult we do not need to use all our senses and move correspondingly in order to find out more about the world. Why? Because we are thinking in different units—we have internalised our early actions and can operate with them in our heads, e.g. we can 'reverse' actions by tracing steps backwards. Thus we use operations in operational thinking (internalised actions)—at first these logical features making up our conceptual system are very 'concrete' —they are concerned with actual objects and situations and reasoning tends to be linked to this concrete reality. In adolescence these operations can become 'formal' as well as 'concrete'—that is we can think in more abstract terms, and reason how hypothetical ideas are linked with the actual—this is the realm of propositions and hypotheses, with thought freed from actual experiences. Clearly not all people reach this stage with any real degree of competence.

What happens between the 'action' stage of sensori-motor thought and the 'operation' stages of concrete and formal logical reasoning? Here is the rub, and the area of most controversy. Briefly, Piaget argues for an elongated period of 'pre-operations' (about five years normally, between say two and seven years of age very roughly) in which the basic schemas are elaborated into images and symbolic thinking starts to develop into concepts. Thinking is not logical, says Piaget, in this transition period—a child might talk 'conservation' because if a display of counters is re-arranged, for instance, a young child may be led to think that the actual number of counters has been altered. Thus he moves from sensori-motor thinking through a period of pre-conceptual thought (where images and symbols are developing) to intuitive thinking (where he is semi-logical because concepts are developing but he can come unstuck easily by the way things appear to him) and then moves into the operational logical stage.

Although the ages are not in any way fixed, the sequence of stages is invariant—the speed of development will be variable, some developing at a quicker rate than others, but everyone is 'programmed' to pass through them in a fixed, invariant order.

This model is a very internally consistent one, based on logical, mathematical type lines. The question is, however, is it 'real'? Does it have any psychological reality? Some very major criticisms have been made in recent years, and whilst many would not wish to dismiss the whole of the Piagetian framework, it would seem that it is due for an extensive overhaul. The following is a list of the types of problems that have been raised: are children illogical or semi-logical at four and five, or can we alter the task to make it more meaningful, within a setting with human meaning and social interaction, and discover that a four-year-old is capable of logical, operational thought? Evidence is building up to show that in fact we can (Bryant, 1974; Donaldson, 1978; Brown and Desforges, 1977). Is Piaget's premise correct that experience being based upon a genetic base causes all children to proceed through the same stages—do these stages actually exist, or are they figments of a very consistent, mathematical imagination? In fact some have pointed out that it is difficult to predict future development because there are some very impressive discontinuities in development (having to forget and unlearn things) as well as the well known continuities in development (having to modify and integrate past learning) (Clarke and Clarke, 1976a). Smedslund (1977) has attacked the artificiality and abstract nature of tasks and the status of the structures of the Piagetian practice, and Brown and Desforges (1977) have gathered together many studies which lead them to question the whole notion of general stages of development. Moreover, Piaget gives much emphasis to activity in cognitive development, but as Anthony (1977) has pointed out, many studies have shown that this insistence on physical activity is excessive—children are quite capable of furthering their learning and understanding by observing others at work. These objections are major ones, and if added to the many minor objections (like Piaget's sampling methods and research techniques) then it becomes clear that his model is seriously wrong in certain important respects, and alternative reformulations are necessary—for example, Brown and Desforges (1977) propose a change from stages to a 'skill integration' model of development, and this idea is discussed further in this chapter and in chapter 5.

Is all this academic pie-in-the-sky? So what if Piaget is right or partly right or entirely wrong? We draw some implications for all of this at the end of the chapter, but we can make a general comment here. It should be emphasised that the Piagetian model has lots of support which is fairly uncritical (see Varma and Williams, 1976) and rightly or wrongly it has considerably influenced the school curriculum and will probably continue to do so for many years (with the possible exception of language programmes—see Lunzer, 1976). If we assume that children cannot think logically in the pre-school and early school years—as Piaget would have us believe—and if we design our teaching around this central belief, as we have done, largely—then we are doing a massive injustice to children if they in fact are capable of logical thought (Donaldson, 1978). Piaget also tends to play down the emphasis on language in school and stresses rather activity methods and personal discovery. For him, the ability to use language is the outcome of activity. (He sees a danger in equating the linguistic facility that a highly vocal child may display with an assumption that a system of well developed concepts has been acquired—very talkative children may mislead adults into believing that their powers of conceptual understanding are greater than they actually are!) For many years this belief has informed teaching strategy. He may be wrong, and indeed, as the Bullock Report (1975) stresses, language is a central factor in children's cognitive learning and development. Bruner, as we shall now see, puts this particular house in order.

Bruner's model

Jerome Bruner's work on cognitive growth has followed some general themes since the 1960s. One theme concerns the means by which people 'represent their experience of the world' (1966). He, like Piaget, discusses the remarkably different methods adopted over the period of development. Although there are important differences between Bruner and Piaget, there are also some important points of similarity. Bruner (1964) refers to the progressive mastery of intellectual techniques (or 'tools' from the mental 'toolkit') which we apply in analysing the workings of the world. He refers to these techniques as modes of representational thinking. These are called the enactive mode, the iconic mode and the symbolic mode of representation. Each mode has its own particular way of representing events, and as Bruner emphasises 'each places a powerful impress on the mental life of human beings at different ages, and their interplay persists as one of the major features of adult intellectual life' (Bruner et al., 1966). These are not strictly 'stages' which one moves through and leaves, but a subtle collection of 'techniques' which accumulates with development and which *all* integrate and work together in the adult mind when solving problems.

What are the characteristics of each mode?

1 *Enactive mode* A young infant's world is discovered by the actions he performs in order to cope with it. There are obvious parallels here with Piaget's sensori-motor phase of development when past events are represented through motor responses. So a baby who has dropped a rattle will still represent the rattle by a continuing shaking movement. An object is very much what is done to it. Bruner stresses that, as adults, we still use this enactive mode—try describing your precise movements in taking a shower, driving a car or touch-typing. It is far easier to mime or pretend a situation because these events are more or less 'represented in our muscles'.

2 *Iconic mode* How does a child get from actions, which are relatively slow, to the quicker aspects of thought? For Bruner, the iconic mode is the second major mental system that becomes available as we develop. It is characterised essentially by images (or icon-like features). Thus a child becomes able to represent the world to himself by an image (or visual-schema) that is relatively free from action—he can select and organise his perception and work with 'pictures' which stand for perceptual events. In effect, the imagery is able to summarise action, by the internalised imitations now available. So this is a

very elementary form of symbolisation, and the next mode takes it from here.

3 *Symbolic mode* As adults, we use a number of specialist 'codes' in our lives. These are different systems for representing the business of living in symbols—we look at maps, diagrams, plans, road signs, we read words and numbers, listen to music and of course we speak. The most central system of symbolic activity is language, but not the only one as Bruner points out. This symbolic way of getting along does not just help and reflect life, it translates and transforms our experiences. Bruner says that our experiences are 'amplified'. In so doing, the child has to develop the ability to match language and actions and perceptual images, and this matching process, he argues, needs to be trained with schooling: 'without special training in the symbolic representation of experience, the child grows to adulthood still depending in large measure on the enactive and iconic modes of representing and organising the world, no matter what language he speaks' (Bruner et al., 1966).

Bruner, then, attaches far more importance to centrality of language in the development of intelligence than does Piaget. He also thinks that the cultural experiences are more important in determining and shaping growth. His famous phrase that 'cognitive growth in all its manifestations occurs as much from the outside in as from the inside out' (Bruner et al., 1966) illustrates this, and confirms the interaction view outlined in chapter 3.

Before we move on we should emphasise a conclusion of paramount importance which Bruner draws from his work—given the various modes of knowing the world, and the great importance of cultural influence in development, then rather than wait until a child is educationally 'ready' for some set of tasks, we should find ways of enhancing learning and understanding. We should do this by presenting material and ideas matched as closely as possible to the mode of representation with which they are operating, and we return to this in chapter 5.

What pushes thinking forward?

Again we meet a very large issue hidden in four little words! The question bears many similarities to chapter 3—'What affects intelligence?' Do our intellectual competences increase as the genetic programme unfolds? How important are environmental and cultural pressures? The issue here is not what, but how? Even if we give the environmental factors full causal status, we still need to know just how they work. As Bruner says, 'the "pushes" and "unfoldings" need further specification' (Bruner et al., 1966). What explanations have been advanced?

Piaget (1950) sees intelligence as an adaptive process to the environment. He says that such adaptation has two aspects—assimilation and accommodation. The individual has a set of schemas, concepts and so on. As new experiences come along, he applies this system to enhance understanding. So, existing methods of working can be applied to new situations, and these are absorbed and integrated into the old—they are assimilated. E.g., a child learning to tell the time assimilates all types of conventional clock faces into that particular aspect of telling time. But what happens when this child meets a digital clock or watch? His old methods will not do. His developing system is thrown out of 'equilibrium'. He has to find a new method to solve the problem (and return to equilibrium) or give up altogether! In other words, he cannot assimilate now but has to accommodate—that is change the method or modify existing schemas/concepts. The notion behind this type of explanation is that of cognitive conflict—when a puzzling phenomenon is met, a state of conflict arises, and in resolving this conflict (finding other ways) thinking is pushed forward.

Although there are many problems with this type of explanation, such as its lack of specificity and to an extent its circularity and explanatory power (Bolton, 1972), there is probably something in the notion of cognitive conflict, (Bower, 1974). Hunt has utilised the notion in curriculum design and refers to the 'problem of the match' (1971) and Donaldson (1978) links this notion of cognitive conflict with the desire to learn. We examine this in the next chapter. Bruner also would argue that the mis-match between the modes of representation leads the child into some conflict that has to be resolved—though the stresses the role of the culture more in contriving some conflict to ensure development.

The processes of thinking—another approach

Mussen, Conger and Kagan (1974) and Kagan and Lang (1978) present a different system or organisation for describing the course of intellectual development. This approach puts stress on a number of processes which have been investigated experimentally and which are believed to combine to form the activity of thinking as opposed to the 'stage' approach. (See Ault (1977) for a full comparison of both approaches.) The processes are four in number: (1) perception, (2) memory, (3) generation and testing of hypotheses and (4) evaluation. They manifest themselves at all ages, but develop in complexity as children get older. These processes work on the units of thinking (as outlined earlier in the chapter), just as the digestion process has to have material to process in order to function.

Let us examine each process in turn, though in effect each is involved with the functions of each other and for each important changes take place over time. What is involved in finding answers and solutions to 'problems' which fill our daily lives?

1 perception—this is the process that takes meaningful information from the relatively meaningless mass available, and refers to all the senses, not just vision. Information is taken from the senses, combined with past experiences stored in the memory, and the product arrived at is some very individual 'picture' of a situation. This process entails selective attention—a camera will capture nearly everything in a situation (and this in only one sense-channel–visual)—but a person selects particular items for attention. In other words, in order to extract meaningful information, critical features of an event must be identified, and then matched up with an appropriate unit (e.g. does it fit X or Y concept?), so memory of past experiences is also involved in increasing the understanding of the world.

2 memory—this process involves the storage of experiences for some time after they have occurred. There are a number of research findings which are appropriate here, because 'memory' is perhaps too wide a term. Traditionally we can talk in terms of sensory memory—a storage system which captures a vivid impression of an event for a very brief period, less than one second. After this short-term memory is a slightly longer device which allows the person to hold on to information for up to thirty seconds or so while some initial meaning is attached—for example, remembering the time just long enough to do something with the information. The information must be transferred to the long-term memory store if a longer retention is required, and here the person very actively reformulates, transforms and organises the information according to his individual needs (Gagné, 1977). Craik and Lockhart (1972) proposed a rather different explanation from this traditional three-system approach, and suggested that information is processed at different levels depending on the degrees of analysis made. So, memory can operate at a visual/auditory sensory

level (shapes/sounds), or at the other extreme at a level incorporating complete understanding of material and its integration with existing knowledge (see Riding, 1977, for a fuller discussion).

3 generation and testing of hypotheses (decision-making)—with any problem, one has to perceive that problem—(1) above—and make efficient use of memory—(2) above. But to find a solution, we must 'put up' some possible ideas and answers, and then 'test' these for effectiveness. This process encompasses verbal and non-verbal techniques, and topics such as creativity and learning sets and transfer. The number of ideas generated is largely a function of past experience with similar problems (explaining in part why children tend to get better as they get older). With more cognitive units at a child's disposal (e.g. schemas or concepts) a solution is more probable because more knowledge can be tapped. (Ault, 1977 describes some fascinating work in this area.)

4 evaluation—this process, the least well researched of the four, concerns the child in making a decision about the effectiveness of his behaviour. Does he pause and consider/assess the quality of thinking —does he jump into a solution immediately, with some unthinking impulse, or does he reflect upon possible better alternatives first? This work encompasses Kagan's work on cognitive tempo or learning style (1966). He proposed that children who 'jump in' immediately are impulsive, whereas children who take their time are reflective. This style, it is argued, is closely associated with success at school work, and Kagan has attempted training children to modify their 'conceptual tempo'. Donaldson (1978) discusses the implications of this with reference to cognitive theory and the teaching of reading. Other cognitive styles have been suggested by others, for example, Witken's work (Witkin *et al.*, 1962) on field independence, but Kagan's work is probably most related to aspects of evaluation.

The astute reader will have realised by now that this approach has many similarities with Guilford's 'Three Faces of Intellect' (see chapter 1 and Guilford 1967). However, one difference to note is that the boundaries of these processes are not as clear-cut as Guilford's model would imply. They are inter-related and overlap, and they do not operate in any specific sequence—there may be some parallel processing, as indicated by Ault (1977). Also, the following possibility is worthy of consideration—that the processes which are operating on the structural units (schema, images, concepts) lead to the differing developmental levels (or stages) as described above. For example, as the child generates and tests various hypotheses (ideas) about the meaning of certain concepts, then those concepts might change in meaning, richness, texture, etc. This is shown in figure 4.4.

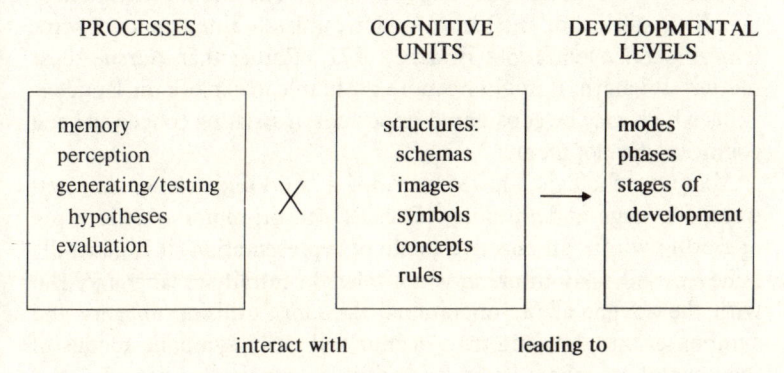

PROCESSES	COGNITIVE UNITS	DEVELOPMENTAL LEVELS

memory
perception
generating/testing
  hypotheses
evaluation
	structures:
	schemas
	images
	symbols
	concepts
	rules
		modes
		phases
		stages of
		  development

interact with		leading to

Figure 4.4 A possible relationship between cognitive processes and cognitive units

Language in cognitive development—some implications

One thing that seems certain is that the function of language in thinking is extremely important, and this is shown in the topics of stages/modes of development, cognitive conflict and intellectual processes all discussed above. It is to this that we finally turn, and in part attempt to bring some specificity into the discussion—just what skills should teachers isolate and concentrate upon in helping to push cognitive development forward? These skills are essentially linguistic, but of course visual and motor skills are also involved. It might become apparent that in many ways the last approach discussed (the alternative view to stages—that of the processes of thinking) is more useful in informing the content of curricula.

There have been many complicated debates about which comes first—language or thinking—and which is more important than the other. Russian psychologists tend to say that both have different roots (Luria and Yudovich, 1959; Vygotsky, 1962); Piaget plays down the part played by language in development and puts emphasis on actions and operations as thinking; Bruner takes another path and says that thought comes to conform to language as the major transformer of experience. Likewise, for accounts of the nature of language—sociologists examine codes of communication as with Bernstein's well-known 'formal' and 'restricted' codes (1961); psycholinguistics may stress the innate nature of language rules (Chomsky, 1968); behavioural psychologists argue that language is essentially a chain of stimulus—response bonds (Osgood, 1957). These arguments tend to be a little sterile and difficult to follow, unless written about at some length (see Lovell, 1968; Francis, 1977). Rather than pursue these matters at length, it might be more profitable to explore the language skills which may be considered important in assisting conceptual and cognitive development.

Many psychologists have described a 'working' relationship between language and thinking. Because sensori-motor functions are operating within an enactive mode of representation, it is generally believed that early thinking is not related centrally to language. But with the advent of pre-operational thinking, utilising imagery and symbolisation (thus inferring iconic and early symbolic modes of representation) then language works to represent, describe and systematically transform experience. This refines the thinking processes and thereby is seen to be a vital technique in setting thinking on a more powerful and economic pathway. Therefore, advances in language lead to advance in cognition (and verbal intelligence possibly). This is shown in figure 4.5.

```
EARLY THOUGHT ⟶ LANGUAGE ⟶ REFINED THOUGHT

sensori-motor          ↓              extensive
  enactive         represents        conceptual
                  describes and       system
                  systematically
                    transforms
                    experience
```

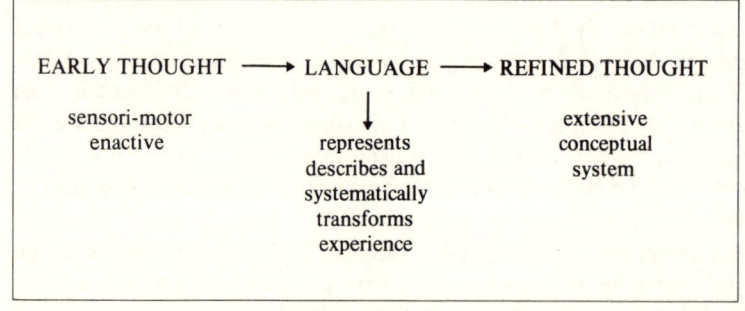

Figure 4.5 Language in thinking

What skills are located in the sphere of language? How can the teacher enhance this movement from early to refined thinking, and thereby optimise the intelligence of children? One useful model, though by no means perfect, is the input-output model as used in the Illinois Test of Psycholinguistic Abilities (see chapter 2). Many writers have taken the principles of the model to make a start on isolating the language skills thought to be of some importance, though non-verbal skills are also included (e.g. Cooper *et al.*, 1978; Bryans and Wolfendale, 1973; Kirk and Kirk, 1971; Wedell, 1973; Leach and Raybould, 1977). This model should not be seen in any way as definitive—we must guard against an oversimplistic approach. With many children it may not be appropriate to analyse and investigate components such as these. It would perhaps be more sensible to stay 'on-task'. For example, if a child is slow in acquiring reading skill, rather than have recourse to investigating 'underlying processes', it might be more beneficial to stay with the reading process and examine the actual reading skill involved. A simple interpretation is shown in Figure 4.6 of a model that can be educationally useful in certain situations.

RECEPTION	PROCESSING	EXPRESSION
receiving and understanding	'inner-language' to integrate and direct behaviour	communicating and expressing
visual and auditory skills of location, attention and discrimination	decision-making processes	using vocabulary and sentences in verbal expression
	memory skills	manual expression
initial understanding	concept formation	
	symbolic processing	
	sensory integration	
	association	
	further understanding	

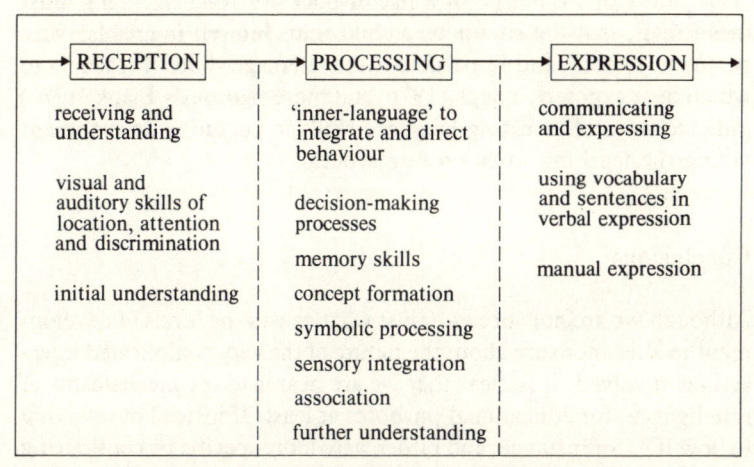

Figure 4.6   A simplified model of cognitive skills in development

If language is to become internalised as a vehicle for thinking, then we might postulate some processes involved and skills required. Using a simple input-output model as shown in figure 4.6 a child must be able to receive successfully the information which he hears (auditory skills of analysis) and sees (visual understanding). Thus he has to attend to the relevant information after locating the source, and successfully analyse and discriminate (or decode). Then this information has to be processed—he has to do things with it (which involves important memory functions, symbol processing and understanding, conceptual development and understanding of situations), integrate all the sensory information and generally develop skills which allow his 'inner language' to integrate and direct his behaviour. He must then be able to communicate and express his ideas, requests, thoughts, etc., and the two ways of doing this are to speak (verbal expression at a number of levels) and/or to use the motor responses of the body (manual expression). Many aspects of this skills model, which are discussed further in the next section, have formed the basis of infant school curricula and remedial programmes (e.g. Bryans and Wolfendale, 1973; Leach and Raybould, 1977).

The approach in this model stresses the view that a child's understanding of the world is not simply a passive reception of information and 'facts', but that rather it is a construction of personal knowledge —that is experience which is re-organised, transformed, amplified by the individual according to particular situations and needs. Francis (1977) develops this line in a useful book for teachers. This must mean then, that the situations a child finds himself in are also very pertinent factors, and in particular the language skills of teachers to which he is exposed. Tough (1976) and more rigorously Blank (1977) indicate ways of assessing language skills in cognitive development taking the teaching situation into acount.

Conclusions

Although we are not sure as to just what causes the levels of development to alter, nor sure about the nature of the very complicated interactions involved, it is clear that we are nearer to the mechanisms of intelligence, for educational purposes at least. If instead of referring to 'low IQ', for instance, and rather were more specific by considering the possibilities discussed in this chapter, then we should be in a much stronger position in helping children move forward.

It is not coincidental that the innovatory measures of intellectual skill discussed in chapter 2 have looked towards approaches outlined in this chapter for a more useful appraisal of abilities. Hunt's work on ordinal scales of behavioural assessment relies heavily on Piaget's structural approach. (We discussed some major criticisms of the Piagetian framework, but did not dismiss the approach out of hand!) The British Ability Scales utilises much from the models of processes discussed here—the processes of thinking (e.g. perception, memory, and so on), the dimensions of formal operational thinking, and the skills involved in the input-output model (see figure 4.6). The ITPA rests entirely on this skills-based approach outlined here. As we shall discuss further in the next chapter, all these measures take what at present is known about the development of intelligence, isolate key skills, and evaluate individual competence in those skills.

Chapter 5

Intelligence and learning

In this chapter we attempt to draw many threads together. The major concern here is to investigate the relationship between intelligence, as examined in previous chapters, and learning in the home and school situations. The first issue is about the notion of 'underachievement', because it is this that utilises, in an often dubious way, the relationship between what a child is doing, and what he is ultimately thought capable of doing. The whole book, in some ways, is about this very issue. We then go on to question these traditional links between IQ and school achievement by examining the events of learning which are entailed in intellectual skills and abilities. These events constitute an analysis of what is actually involved in the learning process and how poor learners differ from good learners. Attempts to describe optimal learning environments are then examined along with some general implications regarding the 'structured' approach to teaching and learning.

Could do better?

Many children without doubt are underperforming at school, in the sense that their levels of educational achievement are below what we might expect of them—this is especially so for children from immigrant families and from low socio-economic homes. But there is much more to this problem than is often recognised, and it is largely tied up with our notions of intelligence. John Holt made a very interesting statement in his book *How Children Fail*. He said children 'fail to develop more than a tiny part of the tremendous capacity for learning, understanding, and creating with which they were born and of which they made full use during the first two or three years of their lives'

(1964). We meet here, however, a conceptual problem which is central to the very real and practical issue of underachievement. The problem revolves around what a child is at present doing and what that child is capable of doing. We are back to where we started in chapter 1 – the distinction between capacity and performance. Capacity might be taken to mean the highest possible level of performance attainable, limited only by size, genetic endowment and so on. In this sense, capacity could represent the learning potential of an individual. Performance is what is actually done at a particular time which is observed and possibly measured. This refers to the level at which an individual responds. (Note the parallel here between Hebb's Intelligences A and B.)

We often infer a capacity-performance gap—we also have to infer Intelligence A from Intelligence B. The central and very practical question, to which intervention projects like Head Start addressed themselves is, to what extent and under what circumstances can performance be changed? Can performance ever reach capacity? What are the limits of performance?

Bortner and Birch (1970) addressed themselves to these central questions. They noted that many researchers in mental retardation 'view cognitive performance as not necessarily providing an accurate reflection of cognitive capacity', because they observed that changes in circumstances (e.g. training, organisation of tasks, social conditions) significantly affected levels of performance. What they are saying, essentially, is that by noting how a child performs on a particular task provides very little evidence as to what he might ultimately be capable of. In practice, many teachers watch how children perform on tasks, and then guess at their future capabilities. This may be a very mistaken strategy, and one which might lead to gross underestimates of ability. To illustrate this point, consider tasks which young children might be asked to perform. Children might fail such tasks and this usually leads one to conclude that they lack the necessary skills and abilities because they cannot do them. Alter the way the tasks are presented and often they become quite capable of giving the correct responses. Donaldson (1978) provides many examples of this, and we consider here one quoted by Bortner and Birch.

They showed young children an object such as a red button, and asked them to select from three alternatives that object which 'belonged'—red lipstick case, blue counter, spool of thread. The young children either selected the red case (because it also was red) or the blue counter (because it also was round). Older children made a functional choice—they decided that the red button 'belonged to' the spool of thread because of the usage properties. The question now is—did the young children not understand this functional relationship between the button and the thread, or did they basically understand but did not see fit to make such a judgment in practice? Bortner and Birch altered certain features of the tasks—the three alternatives this time were a green case, blue cube and a spool of thread. This time the children chose the spool of thread! What happened was *not* that they lacked the ability but that they were responding to perceptual properties in the first instance. This type of study also supports the developmental views to some extent which were discussed in chapter 4.

Thus it is perhaps the case that we should say that a child does not do a task rather than infer that he cannot. This is not pedantic playing with words, but has quite important teaching implications. We should decide not whether a task can ever be accomplished, but when, and by what circumstances we can modify the learning situation to enhance solutions to such problems. This is another way of saying, be careful not to infer capacity (that is X cannot do it) from performance (that is X does not do it). All we can usefully say is that the present performance of an individual does not directly reflect capacity, but rather represents only a fragment of capacity in accordance with the particular task in hand.

What has this capacity-performance discussion to do with the theme of intelligence? It is often taken as gospel that IQ tests, being supposed measures of intelligence, indicate capacity and potential. This is plainly not so for a number of reasons. Following logically from the above argument, all IQ tests can do at the most is to indicate a fragment of possible capacity because they are tapping in some degree present performance in cognitive tasks. Even the idea that IQ tests measure intelligence is a dubious one as we have discussed earlier. However, accepting this limitation we must conclude that capacity as such is not fully indicated by such tests. This again supports Hebb's idea that Intelligence B can only be indirectly measured and that A never can be.

IQ and school achievement

This leads us squarely into another very popular staffroom myth. Put simply, it is that IQ scores indicate 'capacity' (innate potential, even) these scores often found from group verbal and non-verbal tests, and that attainment (reading, maths, spelling etc) is 'performance'. It is but a short step now to another myth—that a discrepancy between IQ and attainment scores indicate 'underachievement'. Thus, in short we have the following line of argument:

IQ = capacity/potential
attainment age = performance
average/high IQ and low attainment = underachievement
IQ and attainment equal = as expected

If we put some figures on this mythical line of argument, then the point probably becomes clearer:

IQ score	Attainment score
120	90 = underachievement
90	70 = underachievement
120	115 = as expected
100	97 = as expected
75	75 = as expected

There are a number of inter-connected faults to point out here. First, we have a logical flaw as discussed above—we cannot infer capacity directly, and certainly not by using a very rough group IQ score. Second, we may be asking sensible questions about the educational performance of a child with very high IQ and low attainment scores. However, the strategy followed allows us to rest on our laurels for those children with not such a wide discrepancy. This is quite unacceptable because average or low performance should not be expected just because the IQ parallels such attainment. It may be that most children are underfunctioning (attainments not being as high as they might be) and that this just becomes more pronounced and noticeable at the extremes. Third, largely because IQ does successfully predict school success, people have slipped into thinking that IQ causes successful attainment. This is a well-known scientific slip—because two things are correlated this does not allow us to announce that one is causing the other. There may be one or more other factors operating, which we consider below. IQ and attainment tests, as Vernon (1970) and Humphreys (1971) have shown, are both types of achievement test. The fourth problem is that of the overachiever! Yule, Rutter and Berger (1974) have shown that in a large-scale study of IQ and reading scores, there were as many children with Reading Ages above their IQ levels as there were below! That is, there were as many overachievers as underachievers. How, then, can children be performing beyond their capacity? Clearly the notion is faulty. Technically, what is required to estimate attainment scores from IQ scores is the use of a 'regression' equation. This is because of a well-known effect which shows that the correlation between IQ and attainment is not perfect, but is around 0·6. Therefore, IQ and attainment scores cannot even be expected to be parallel. To predict attainment from IQ one needs to account for this imperfect relationship by using a regression equation—this permits one to predict the value of one score (e.g. reading) on the basis of another (e.g. IQ), but taking into account the imperfect relationship between the two sources. Even by using this equation, however, the mythical beliefs discussed are still quite pertinent, and as Vernon (1970) and Brody and Brody (1976) forcefully point out, the main culprits in upholding these beliefs are often professional psychologists!

So what can we safely and sensibly say about IQ, achievement and underachievement? Vernon (1968) provides a useful approach. He notes that both IQ and attainment tests are both measuring different types of achievement—for IQ tests this amounts to generalised thinking skills, and for attainment tests more specific skills. Thus, it is quite possible for a child to score lower or higher on IQ than on attainment, just as one could do better on English than on Maths. Humphreys (1971) reiterates this central point when he states that 'items in all psychological and educational tests measure acquired behaviour'. When low IQ and low attainment are found, then the IQ itself needs explaining, and we look at this later on in the chapter. Vernon goes on to state that 'equally, a good IQ cannot be accepted as measuring potentiality in the sense of showing the maximum that the child might achieve if he had been brought up in a more favourable environment or been better taught'. However, we would be silly to abandon the belief of children 'not working up to capacity'. Thus he says that 'we must think out afresh how we can employ notions of potentiality and underfunctioning' (1968).

Basically, Vernon is pleading for much more than IQ to be taken into account when describing, diagnosing, treating and making prognosis in underachievement. Four essential features should be taken into account:

(1) IQs do give a good sample of general intellectual functioning, but there are discrepancies. An all round assessment of a child's verbal and non-verbal abilities, school attainment and behaviour in everyday life should be undertaken. Underfunctioning would be suspected if a 'marked unevenness' were observed. So we must relate to a pattern

of abilities.

(2) Since we know of factors which can retard performance, a survey of personal circumstances should be carried out (a mini case study) in order to link the ability pattern with background factors.

(3) We must have evidence of remediability—that is evidence that modifications of these circumstances if possible at all would lead to an improvement. In this respect, we discuss the idea of 'mini-learning experiments' later in the chapter.

(4) All the above considerations must be based on 'clinical' judgments—weighing up the ability and circumstances of a particular case.

So, we seem to use an IQ figure mistakenly—just one 'single-shot' sample of behaviour—and from this predict potential behaviour. We have discussed this problem in general terms in chapter 3. Educational performances, and therefore difficulties, are rarely the result of one cause or factor alone. Almost invariably, because children are not simple creatures, a multiplicity of interacting and interdependent factors are involved. This must involve non-intellectual factors such as personality and motivation. For a useful discussion on this, see Rutter (1975). It could be that we are 'over-predicting' achievement on an IQ basis rather than the child actually 'underachieving'. As Thorndike (1963) makes clear, 'As a research problem, the problem of underachievement is one of understanding our failures in predicting achievement and of identifying more crucial factors or additional factors that will permit us to predict more accurately'. Donaldson (1963) makes a sound and very pertinent point. After discussing issues in predicting ability, she asks,

> How, then, would it be reasonable to make use of tests of intelligence if it is allowed that the development of ability may not be wholly pre-determined, and unaffected by our decisions and actions? The implication would seem to be that they should be used not so much for long-term as for very immediate prediction. It would be reasonable to use them to tell us what a child is ready to go on to *now*, to indicate whether we can expect him, in his present stage of development, to start successfully on this or that new attempt at learning.

Intellectual abilities and learning

One central point discussed in the last section was that intelligence and achievement (and the related tests) are not qualitatively different—this serves to highlight a view held by some that intelligence and learning are overlapping concepts (e.g. McFarland, 1971). Many have pointed out, often with more than a hint of cynicism, that years of research have been devoted to statistical psychometric investigations into assessing individual differences, but attempts to locate the sources of difference have been sadly lacking (Brody and Brody, 1976). We have made lots of descriptions and found relatively few leads to mechanisms which highlight causes. In fact it is worse than this, as we have previously noted, since often the descriptions (e.g. IQ figures) have been set up as explanations with the labelling of people as more or less intelligent, and this being accepted as a cause of their behaviour. (Why does he act as he does? Because he is very bright).

What we badly need to do now is to go beyond statistical description and get at some processes—not to go on and on talking about low IQ's, for instance, but to find out why they are not higher, what is causing the IQ to be low, can we train up those functions and processes, whatever they may be, to improve thinking skills and work out specific instructional programmes to suit individual requirements? We made a start in this direction, developmentally, in chapter 4. However, there is no one way of going about this, as Labouvie-Vief (1976) points out—one method is to look at notions of 'abilities', as discussed in chapter 1, and search for 'anchor points in current formulations of learning processes'. In other words, we need to get away from looking at one line of evidence (e.g. the IQ) and use many more lines, because ability is more than a statistical result from correlational analysis. Humphreys (1971) describes an attempt to go beyond intelligence testing as a way forward in understanding intelligence and examines some possible hypotheses from learning, genetics and developmental studies. Similarly, Howe (1975) attempts 'to show how learning processes are closely involved in the events that lead to human development and a child's acquisition of crucial abilities'. Anastasi (1970), Rapier (1962), Guilford (1967) and many others have stressed that we should relate traditional notions of ability to learning processes and also to the work on the development of intellectual abilities as outlined in chapter 4. Resnick (1976) has noted that we have often not been successful in identifying 'situations in which one instructional treatment was best for individuals of one type, as measured by aptitude or ability tests, and a different treatment best for individuals of another type' (known as ability-instruction interactions). The call here is for a blending of experimental and differential psychology to find out which processes are involved in which teaching situations, and which processes individuals could utilise—'there must be a joining of psychometric and experimental psychology in order to determine the kinds of basic processes that underlie intelligent performance'. Resnick's book of collected papers is a direct response to this—the emphasis has been moved to what intelligence *is*, rather than who *has* it. Work from information-processing, developmental and experimental psychologists is brought together in an attempt to re-examine the notion of intelligence, and many points raised in this book are examined at length in Resnick (1976). Thus to proceed, we need to bring all the previous chapters together—a task of mammoth proportions! All we can do here is to describe some *possibilities* which might be of educational interest.

Events in learning

An argument was developed earlier in the book emphasising the genetic and environmental interactions and transactions which are central in the developing abilities and intellectual skills of children. What learning environments will enhance such transactions and what is actually involved in the act of learning? If we can find answers to such questions we shall be better informed in realising whatever potentials for development children possess. The ability to learn is without doubt influenced considerably by past learning achievements, and Staats (1971) argues that intelligent children have learned the skills that are involved in intelligent behaviour. They have, therefore, a good basis for further skills acquisition. Similarly, he refers to a 'downward spiral'—children lacking successful learning will have a poor basis for further learning. Howe (1976) examines the differences between poor learners and good learners, and concludes that good learners have 'acquired a set of intellectual skills that vary in function and complexity, so that when faced with new tasks [they are] likely to have available appropriate tools to facilitate learning'.

What, then, constitute the events in learning? Can we isolate these and provide opportunities for learning at home and school which will enhance success and minimise failure? It is in these terms that it is probably the most sensible way of thinking about children learning to be intelligent, or more accurately, learning to display intelligent behaviour.

'Learning' is generally defined as a process (meaning a series of events or changes) in which a form of behaviour is more or less permanently modified as a result of some experience(s). R. M. Gagné in his writings has provided an immensely useful analysis of what is involved in such a process and how the analysis can be applied to teaching and curriculum design. We now look briefly at his main themes. For a more detailed account, see Gagné (1974, 1977) and Gagne and Briggs (1974).

Gagné isolates eight phases in learning and to each can be attributed a specific process. Implications for instruction and teaching accompany each phase. Table 5.1 summarises the major points. Many of these phases are often overlooked or taken for granted in teaching; it would be beneficial in many instances to look at the learning skills of individual children and ask whether certain aspects of their learning can be improved. The following framework can be very useful in this respect.

Table 5.1   Summary of Gagné's phases and processes of learning

	Phase of learning	Associated process	Teaching points
1	Motivation	Expectancy	Inform of objectives Teacher relationship Extrinsic/intrinsic
2	Apprehending	Attention: Selective perception	Direct attention Clear instructions
3	Acquisition	Coding Short-term memory	Hook-up new to old learning
4 5	Retention/Recall	Long-term memory Retrieval	Encourage use of cues; revision strategies
6	Generalisation	Transfer of learning	Apply bones of one situation to another
7 8	Performance Feedback	Responding Reinforcement	Encourage responding Provide accurate and precise feedback. Ensure feelings of success.

1 Initially, a learner should be motivated. A good way to achieve this is to establish expectancy—for example, by providing incentives to start. Ideally, motivation should be intrinsic, that is the task itself

should be of the correct level of interest and difficulty in order to 'turn the learner on'. Hunt (1971) discusses this idea of intrinsic motivation, which is involved in what he refers to as the 'problem of the match' which we return to later. At first, however, some extrinsic motivation may be required—the use of some tangible reward, perhaps, if the task is begun or finished. In addition, informing children of goals or rewards will help. The crucial factor of the positive relationship between the teacher (or parent) and the learner must not be overlooked.

2 Once motivation is established, a learner must attend to the relevant stimuli of the situation, and this involves selecting the relevant features from the irrelevant. Many attempts to learn fail largely because attention is inappropriately directed (see Ross, 1976).

3 This is probably the most important phase–if the material is to be acquired it must be coded meaningfully at this point for successful processing later. A learner must be able to link up the new experience with his previous learning and understanding or the immediate relevance will be lost (see the discussion on short term memory in chapter 4). The teacher can provide many ways to help children hook up new material to that which is already grasped and understood.

4 and 5 These phases involve other aspects of memory, which again were discussed in chapter 4. The learner, having successfully coded information, has to store this in long term memory, and when required has to recall it by retrieval techniques. As previously emphasised, though, this is not a mechanical process. The learner does not passively file information away, but makes decisions about it, organises it according to past experience, reformulates and transforms it. This active involvement in learning is a view supported strongly by research discussed in chapter 3 (e.g. the transactional model) and in chapter 4 (e.g. Bruner's work).

6 A good learner is able to take the bones out of one situation and apply these to similar situations—he generalises his learning and this involves the notion of learning transfer. This has been referred to as 'learning how to learn' (Harlow, 1949), and involves applying the same principles in a variety of situations. Many curriculum projects encourage children to do this. Indeed, Ferguson (1954) considered intelligence not as a nebulous thing that we have because of some mysterious means, but as generalised techniques of learning and thinking which have developed out of experiences. Such 'habits' which we learn transfer to a variety of problems and become overlearned due to much practice. Those involved with children should

try to promote such skills of learning transfer as much as possible.

7 and 8 How do we know that learning has been accomplished? The only certain way is to have the correct responses demonstrated and the more we allow children to show these correct responses the better. After responding, feedback is necessary. A learner must know how he got on—not in vague terms, but in specific terms which can be more useful. The informational nature of this point is crucial, and in this respect appropriate reinforcement will serve a number of functions—e.g. provide information for the nature of errors, enhance further motivation and so on. Teachers can always transmit feelings of success and reduce those of failure in order to establish and consolidate positive and effective learning processes.

Another important aspect of Gagné's analysis is that of learning outcomes—the results of acts of learning. Learning outcomes mean that one possesses specifiable learned capabilities. What are these? Gagné identifies basically three areas of outcome—(1) *knowledge* (verbal information, resulting in knowing 'this and that' like names and facts). (2) *attitudes,* both those toward learning itself, and the cognitive strategies which a learner adopts to manage his own learnings. (3) *skills* which are of two types: motor (physical actions) and intellectual (mental 'know-how'). It is the latter category—intellectual skills—with which we are mainly concerned in this book, and here we meet again the notion of hierarchy which we met in chapter 4 (see figure 4.1). Intellectual skills proceed from simple discriminations (distinguishing the differences between two objects, situations, etc) through concepts to rule and higher order rules. Unlike the developmental approach—see chapter 4—Gagné does not use terms like stages of development in intellectual skill. Instead of writing in terms of stage endings and beginnings that 'determine' when a child is 'ready' for a particular task, he simply states that the present capabilities of an individual determine what is appropriate to learn next. This is the essential meaning of a hierarchy (or vertical organisation) of skill, and it is of course the rationale behind criterion-referenced measurements (see chapter 2). The intellectual skills and the cognitive strategies adopted by the learner lead into the study of problem solving and creative learning. Likewise, the work on 'artificial intelligence' and attempts to describe a 'General Problem Solver' (GPS) are computerised attempts at becoming more specific in the analysis of learning outcomes which Gagné describes (see Butcher, 1968; Annett, 1974).

Gagné's analysis of learning has much in common with other

models and approaches discussed in this book. It is not unlike Guilford's ideas (see chapter 1) and the ITPA model (see chapter 2) and the process approach to cognitive development (see chapter 4) and figure 4.6 bears some resemblance. Writers such as Bijou (1976), Bruner (1964), Staats (1971), Bloom (1956) and Klausmeier (1976) refer to such an analysis either directly or indirectly, and even the attempts to reformulate Piaget's model in terms of a 'skill integration model' (Brown and Desforges, 1977) bears similarity in certain aspects. What is this leading up to? It is leading to a position that allows us legitimately to view a child as a developing learner who is active in his own learning, whose intellectual abilities are not fixed for all time early in life, and where positive steps may be taken by adults to enhance the acquisition of learned intellectual skills. Mastery learning is an extreme view of this position, and we examine this next.

Mastery learning

Convention has it that in schools both pupils and teachers expect that only a few will achieve high attainment and achievement, and that most will do fairly well and a few will do badly. In other words we tend to carry in our heads a normal distribution curve not only for intelligence but also for school learning! Bloom and his colleagues (see Block, 1971) state that these assumptions and sorts of expectations tend to fix the goals and objectives of pupils and teachers (and possibly parents) at lowish levels, with a result that often motivation is low. This is often accompanied by class teaching or large-group methods with most children expected to learn the same material at the same pace. Indeed, selection into streams/sets/groups, etc. based upon IQ is common practice and is done such that the classifications made allow class teaching to be more effective. If however the methods and rate of teaching can vary among learners, Bloom maintains that more can become successful in their learning. One way of accomplishing this is by individual and small group instruction.

Mastery learning, then, means that if such conditions can be provided, then 90 to 95 per cent of pupils can actually attain levels which only a few are normally expected to reach. Mastery learning principles reject the idea that children learn under the dictates of a normal curve. The emphasis moves to finding out why X cannot reach mastery on some task which has been previously defined, and away from an assumption that learning is held back because of limited IQ. This view is very much in sympathy with notions of criterion-referenced measurement discussed in chapter 2. In Mastery learning pupils are required to demonstrate knowledge of a specific skill before going to the next skill. The assumption made in this model is that the degree of learning is a function of the time allowed to be spent on the task, and the level of motivation that a pupil brings to the task, and not a function of 'ability'. This approach emphasises the nature of the attitudes which children bring to learning, and along with this a sense of personal effectiveness and positive view of one's own worth ('self-concept' and 'self-esteem'). Clearly, the attitudes of teachers are paramount! The emphasis is away from IQ and towards the Gagné-type approach to an analysis of learning along with criterion-referenced evaluations to monitor progress (often called diagnostic or developmental teaching).

Mastery learning is a particular philosophy which embodies many of the ideas discussed in this book (and consequently rejects other views!) What can be said more generally about the enhancement of learning?

Optimal learning environments

'The question that must be asked', writes Margaret Donaldson, 'and considered seriously, and reconsidered as knowledge and circumstances change, is whether the school experience really is good for our children—as good as we could make it' (1978). She notes further that the early enthusiasm and promise which many young children display often remains unfulfilled, and suggests that the skills valued by the educational system (which are often encapsulated in the concept of 'IQ') may be alien to the 'spontaneous modes of the human mind'. Apart from the evidence which she presents in her splendid book, and which she relates to strategies in the teaching of reading, what other research can be examined which has attempted to maximise children's enthusiasm and curiosity for learning (note the section in chapter 3— 'Attempts to raise IQ'), and what major teaching points seem to emerge?

We have made many points of reference to these questions already —the importance of language in building up a sound conceptual system; the usefulness of examining sets of intellectual skills (rather than adopting solely a generalised view of intelligence); the examination of criterion behaviours with respect to these skills in diagnostic teaching; the attitudes of teachers and parents towards a child's active role in the transactions of his own development (which is as variable as it is consistent); the methods of analysing components of the learning process and using these to maximise teaching effectiveness. One aspect, however, seems to run through all these points—that which we might label *structure in learning*. We discuss this topic now, and would view it as an important component in the total teaching process.

Structure is here used to refer specifically to a systematic approach to the teaching situation (as compared to an over-intuitive, trial and error, 'leaving learning to chance' approach). It involves long-term goal setting and working towards this end using realistic short-term objectives (which are, as far as possible, measurable). It involves systematic, ongoing, diagnostic evaluation (compare criterion-referenced measurement) which provides the learner with knowledge of his results and feedback with a high informational content. It is concerned to enhance learning using the appropriate type of reinforcement, the most beneficial being encapsulated in intrinsic motivation. It requires the material to be learned to be organised in such a way (probably hierarchically) that allows the learner optimal opportunity to 'latch-on' to its meaning and significance. In short, a structured approach means that teachers (and learners) know where they are going, in broad terms, enables them to work towards more immediate objectives, and necessitates the organisation of the learning environment on systematic lines. Behind all these ideas lies the notion of vertical organisation of intellectual skills—the hierarchical growth of skill so often referred to in various guises in this book. Many psychologists have, in their own distinctive way, written of the benefits of organising learning to match this view of development and learning.

Hunt (1971) refers to the 'problem of the match'. By this he means finding the right level of incongruity between present learning capabilities and the task in hand, so that a child will become curious about that task, will become interested, and will be induced to learn. If the task presented is too easy, he may soon become bored; if too difficult he may become frustrated. If we can solve the problem of matching the task to the right level of cognitive complexity and demand, then we are structuring the learning situation to maximum effect, finding levels is the secret, and involved centrally is the principle of intrinsic motivation. (Curiously, Hunt relies heavily on Piaget's work in that he works within the hierarchical structure of knowledge and skill.

Although we might accept hierarchical ideas for educational reasons, this does not mean that we have to agree with Piaget's formulations in their entirety, as we discussed in chapter 4.)

Bruner in a number of his books refers to the importance of structure (e.g. 1960; 1964; 1966). He refers to structure as the key to learning transfer—that is learning a way of thinking. He would like to see the school curriculum organised such that the relationships between tasks can be readily grasped and understood, and this means organising learning in terms of concepts, principles and ideas. Thus, the tasks need to be hierarchically and sequentially organised, and in such a way to enhance understanding and promote discovery and enquiry (but sensibly so!) in the appropriate mode of representation which suits a particular child (see chapter 4). Meaningless repetition of isolated bits of learning is held to be uneconomic. Central to his belief in structure are his notions of (1) curiosity, (2) competence, and (3) reciprocity (1966).

1 Reinforcing Hunt's position, Bruner notes that children respond well to novelty and find attraction to situations which are marginally unfinished or uncertain—this 'imbalance' could be used to harness their curiosity and enhance learning. Structured play is an important aspect of this. Stott (1978a) describes some fascinating work (based on a collection of articles by Bruner, Jolly and Sylva, 1976) which in a clearly defined and structured way harnesses children's play, using games, to their development of motivation and learning.

2 Bruner again reinforces the views discussed earlier when he says that 'we get interested in what we get good at' (Bruner *et al.*, 1966)—we need to feel that we are competent and have some control over the situations we find ourselves in. In this respect, he argues that teachers may be identified by children as models of competence, and in trying to emulate teacher attitudes towards learning, children may enhance their own levels of competence.

3 Also involved is a need to respond to other people and work with others towards a common goal—this reciprocity in social terms is another central aspect in maximising learning.

Bijou (1969, 1976) outlines a general teaching strategy, based upon an extensive 'applied behavior analysis'. Emphasising that the strategy is not 'closed', he recognises that constant modification and revisions are required, and that teaching should be individualised. This is an important point to clarify, and he sensibly does this: 'Individualisation does not mean that all school activities are to be carried out on a one-teacher-to-one-child basis; but it does mean arranging each teaching situation so that a child is practically always responding to material at his own level of competence, or somewhat above, and is always responsive to the contingencies being employed' (1976). His general strategy comprises five basic steps:

1 Specify teaching goals in observable terms.

2 Begin teaching at the child's level of competence, and emphasis here is towards criterion-referenced measurement, rather than IQs.

3 Arrange the teaching situation (materials, procedure, instructions, etc) to facilitate learning in ways that enhance the individuality of a child.

4 Monitor learning progress and alter the situation to advance learning.

5 Follow methods which generalise, elaborate and maintain the behaviours required.

Although Bijou takes a strong behaviourist position, which emphasises that *only* observable responses may be referred to, there are many points here which have been discussed before, and which specify the structured approach in maximising learning.

Previously we have referred to the idea of a mini-learning experiment. Leach and Raybould (1977) in discussing specific approaches to children with learning difficulty support the idea of systematically structuring the learning situation. They argue that we need objective evidence, obtained from real-life situations, to help us gauge how a child will profit from instruction, and also we need to know the means by which a child learns effectively. The answers to these questions—how much teaching is required and how is learning accomplished?—are central in attempting to optimise the learning environment for all children. One way to find answers is to devise a miniature learning experiment, and Leach and Raybould (1977) outline an interesting procedure which incorporates many points already raised in this chapter. Briefly, four basic stages are involved:

1 Determine exactly what is to be taught—what should the child attend to, what must he do.

2 Determine precisely what can and what cannot be done at present on the desired task (compare again criterion-referenced measurement)—this provides the base-line from which to work and gauge progress.

3 Attempt experimental teaching—change the method of teaching or vary procedures within the same method. A conceptual model of a learning system is discussed which provides a useful framework for experimental teaching. It is essentially an 'input-output' model, with

central mediating processes, and incorporates many features already examined (see figures 2.4, 4.6 and table 5.1). As for example, one could try altering the mode of input and/or output (e.g. change from an auditory to visual presentation of material, and encourage more motor and less vocal responses); another is to isolate a particular skill area—e.g. memory—and concentrate on this aspect; examine the other phases in learning and experiment with a greater emphasis on those perhaps previously taken for granted (e.g. more information given when feeding back the performance of a child).

4 Evaluate the extent of change and assess implications for subsequent teaching.

It is apparent that within this structured approach, the notions of individualised learning and experimental teaching are centrally important.

What evidence do we have which supports the concepts being advanced? (For an interesting review of structured teacher behaviour, see Pilling and Pringle, 1978) One line to consider here is the effectiveness of curriculum projects based on a structured approach—e.g. Bruner's *Man—A Course of Study* (MACOS) (1970); *Science 5–13*; *Concept 7–9*. (See, for example, Fontana (1978) for a discussion of such projects, and for aspects of evaluation, see Stenhouse (1975) and Golby et al. (1975).) For more experimental evidence we must turn to carefully controlled studies. Caldwell (1967) reviews some evidence and concludes that 'the conservatism inherent in our present avoidance of carefully designed social action programmes for the very young child needs to be re-examined'. After a series of studies on learning and cognitive development, Staats, Brewer and Gross (1970) conclude that 'the present evidence speaks in favour of early cognitive teaching and against the passive approach to child rearing suggested by the maturational unfolding conception of child development'. Karnes, Teska and Hodgins (1970) evaluates the effects of four programmes of classroom intervention, directed towards the intellectual development of disadvantaged four-year-olds. They found that the most effective was a highly structured experimental programme which made cognitive demands by requiring the linking of visual and motor skills involved in tasks to verbalisations— as the researchers state, 'as the child visually and motorically assessed the correctness of his thinking, he was required to make appropriate verbalizations at every stage of task involvement' (1970). Marion Blank's work suggests this approach in encouraging children to use language in organising their environment (e.g. Blank and Solomon, 1969; Blank,

1973). Bereiter and Engelmann (1966) used a highly structured, drill-like approach with disadvantaged pre-schoolers aimed to increase vocabulary and extend grammatical competence. Their approach is based very much on the general teaching strategy of Bijou (see above) and high gains in both IQ and in basic educational skills have been reported (e.g. Farnham-Diggory, 1972). Garber and Heber (1977) in reporting on their highly successful prevention project (see chapter 3) have stressed the emphasis they gave to a cognitive-language orientation which was implemented via a structured environment on a prescriptive teaching basis.

Although most of these studies relate to young children, the broad principles of structure can be applied quite successfully to teaching and learning at almost all educational levels—for example, Skemp's work on schematic learning (1962, 1971) and Feuerstein (1971) has reported on large changes in personal adjustment and intellectual and cognitive skills achieved by disadvantaged adolescents who had undertaken a specially structured and intense programme of intervention. We reiterate that the broad principles outlined above will benefit all children (not only young and/or disadvantaged) if applied to their learning situations.

Donaldson does not accept it as 'inevitable that only a small majority of people can ever develop intellectually to a high level of competence' (1978). She argues that schools are too concerned with rank-order and force children often to 'disembody' their thinking from situations involving human sense and meaning, and develop skills in abstract isolation. Rather, we should harness their desire for curiosity and use cognitive conflict in a positive fashion that leads to high self-esteem and a further desire for competence and effectiveness. Adopting a rigid attitude towards the hypothetical construct we call intelligence, and supposed measures of it (called IQs) (although useful for certain purposes) will not help one iota in accomplishing these objectives. Teachers and parents are in a strong position to alter learning environments, to design instructional procedures and materials (which can be prescriptive, negotiated, or both) and work towards helping children develop whatever potentials they possess. We have argued here for a structured approach to this end. However, we must emphasise that if those who 'instruct' do not believe in what they are doing, then all will be to no avail, and those 'instructed' will fail to learn, or will learn despite the system we design.

Further Reading

The following books have been selected from the many sources available. They may be useful for more advanced and/or extensive reading on topics and themes discussed in this book.

Brody, E. B. and Brody, N. (1976), *Intelligence—Nature, Determinants and Consequences*, New York, Academic Press.

This book looks selectively at some of the important issues in intelligence. Certain models of the intellect are discussed in some depth, for example Guilford's work, and the relationship of IQ scores to many forms of achievement are outlined. Genetic and environmental factors are reviewed, and the book concludes with a highly critical discussion of the use of IQ tests in educational situations.

Butcher, H. J. (1968), *Human Intelligence—Its Nature and Assessment*, London, Methuen.

This is a most suitable book for those wishing to read further in the traditional topics of intelligence. Although now a little dated, it is quite comprehensive and was written with the intention of emphasising 'intelligence' as a fundamental topic in psychology.

Donaldson, M. (1978), *Children's Minds*, Glasgow, Collins.

An extremely readable and insightful book. Donaldson's thesis is that young children's powers of reasoning are far more developed than Piaget's interpretation (not his theory, as such) would have us believe. This has immense educational implications. She discusses children's failure in school, and relates this to a mis-match between their 'actual' modes of thinking and the relatively low expectactions of competence that teachers tend to have. This theme is centrally related to themes discussed in this present book.

Ginsburg, H. (1972), *The Myth of the Deprived Child: Poor Children's Intellect and Education*, Englewood Cliffs, New Jersey, Prentice Hall

An interesting and critical book, written with some panache. Ginsburg describes and evaluates psychological research and theory concerning poor children's thinking, and in so doing is especially damning of IQ testing. Intelligence is discussed within the context of poor children's functioning and their failure in the American educational system.

Guilford, J. P. (1967), *The Nature of Human Intelligence*, New York, McGraw Hill.

This book attempts to 'give to the concept of "intelligence" a firm, comprehensive and systematic theoretical foundation'. Guilford develops his own model of intelligence, and in doing so provides an extensive and detailed discussion of many studies relating to the various perspectives and approaches discussed briefly in this book (e.g. psychometric, behavioural, biological, developmental and so on). A useful and very comprehensive book.

Sattler, J. M. (1974), *Assessment of Children's Intelligence*, Philadelphia, W. B. Saunders.

An extensive and erudite exposition of individually administered tests of intelligence (mainly the Staford-Binet and Wechsler tests). The discussion ranges over diagnostic applications of tests to topics such as Childhood Schizophrenia and Mental Retardation, and a useful section on psychological reports and consultation is included. A book for the specialist.

Vernon, P. E. (1969), *Intelligence and Cultural Environment*, London, Methuen.

A compact volume which draws together many important points and features of Vernon's writings up to the late sixties. Early chapters summarise cogently many salient issues, and work across many cultures follows. A readable and informative book.

Conference papers and collections of readings

Block, N. and Dworking, G. (eds) (1977), *The IQ Controversy*, London, Quartet Books.

A large selection of critical readings collected together by two philosophers. The collection ranges over the technical aspects of IQ testing, and examines the reliability and validity of measures. The genetic component of IQ differences is debated, and the wider political and social consequences of this are discussed. The editors round off the volume with a 130-page philosophical essay on 'IQ, Heritability and Inequality'.

Butcher, H. J. and Lomax, D. E. (eds) (1972), *Readings in Human Intelligence*, London, Methuen.

Twenty-two readings which sample the important writings on most of the issues discussed in this book. It is a companion volume to Butcher's 1968 book, *Human Intelligence* (see above).

Cancro, R. (ed.) (1971), *Intelligence—Genetic and Environmental Influences*, New York, Grune & Stratton.

A collection of papers based on an American *academic* conference which closely followed Jensen's 1969 paper (see references). This paper triggered off a heated debate, both political and academic, and this conference took place in a climate of 'apprehension, fear and threat', according to the editor. Cancro stresses, however, that this book is not a political document. It is a serious academic debate which examines the theory and measurement of intelligence, and the genetic and environmental factors associated.

Dockrell, W. B. (ed.) (1970), *On Intelligence*, London, Methuen.

In the introduction to this collection of papers (which are the result of a Canadian Symposium which took place in the Spring of 1969), Dockrell poses the question, 'Does the notion of intelligence still help forward our thinking about learning . . . and does it help in our planning for teaching and learning?' This collection, with all the 'big names' like Burt, Vernon, Jensen, Cattell, goes some way in discussing this central question both for psychology and for education.

Eysenck, H. J. (ed.) (1973), *The Measurement of Intelligence*, Lancaster, Medical and Technical Publishing Co.

As the title indicates, this collection of readings is specifically about the measurement of intelligence in the first instance. It extends, however, to relate issues such as types of intelligence, heredity and environment, and intelligence and social class. Eysenck provides an introduction for each section which contains papers from both well-known and relatively obscure sources.

Resnick, L. B. (ed.) (1976), *The Nature of Intelligence*, Hillsdale, New Jersey, Lawrence Erlbaum Associates.

An extremely useful collection of papers based on a 1974 American conference. It reflects (a) the varied viewpoints associated with cognitive and adaptive processes involved in intelligence, and (b) how these processes are related, or thought to relate, to IQ tests. The types of papers are rather different in form and content than papers from the other conferences listed above, perhaps reflecting a move from traditional views and towards more innovatory ideas discussed in this present book.

Bibliography

Akhurst, B. A. (1970), *Assessing Intellectual Ability*, London, English Universities Press.
Anastasi, A. (1958), 'Heredity, environment, and the question "how?"', *Psychological Review*, 65, 197–207.
Anastasi, A. (1965), *Individual Differences*, London, Methuen.
Anastasi, A. (1970), 'On the formation of psychological traits', *American Psychologist*, 25, 899–910.
Annett, J. (1974), 'Intelligent Behaviour', *An Introduction to Psychology*, Unit 14, Milton Keynes, Open University.
Anthony, W. S. (1977), 'Activity in the learning of Piagetian operational thinking', *British Journal of Educational Psychology*, 47, 18–24.
Ault, R. L. (1977), *Children's Cognitive Development*, New York, Oxford University Press.
Ausubel, D. P. (1968), *Educational Psychology—A Cognitive View*, New York, Holt, Rinehart & Winston.

Ballard, P. B. (1922), *Group Tests of Intelligence*, University of London Press.
Bartlett, F. C. (1932), *Remembering*, Cambridge University Press.
Bayley, N. (1949), 'Consistency and variability in the growth of intelligence from birth to eighteen years', *Journal of Genetic Psychology*, 75, 165–96.
Bereiter, C. and Engelmann, S. (1966), *Teaching Disadvantaged Children in the Pre-school*, New Jersey, Prentice-Hall.
Bernstein, B. (1961). 'Social structure, language, and learning', *Educational Research*, iii, 163–76.
Berry, J. W. and Dasen, P. R. (eds) (1974), *Culture and Cognition: Readings in Cross-Cultural Psychology*, London, Methuen.
Bijou, S. W. (1969), 'Promoting optimum learning in chidren', in Wolff, P. and Mackeith, R. (eds), *Planning for Better Learning* (Clinics in Developmental Medicine, 33), London, Spastics Society/Heinemann Medical, 58–67.
Bijou, S. W. (1976), *Child Development: The Basic Stage of Early Childhood*, New Jersey, Prentice-Hall.
Binet, A. (1909), *Les idées modernes sur les enfants*, Paris, Ernest Flammarion.
Binet, A. and Simon, T. (1905), 'Methodes nouvelles pour le diagnostic du niveau intellectuel des anormaux', *L'Année psychologie*, 11, 191–224.

Blank, M. (1973), *Teaching learning in the preschool: A dialogue approach*, Columbus, Ohio, Charles E. Merrill.
Blank, M. (1977), 'Language, the child, and the teacher: a proposed assessment model', in Horn, H. L. Jr and Robinson, P. A. (eds), *Psychological Processes in Early Education*, New York, Academic Press.
Blank, M. and Solomon, F. (1969), 'How shall the disadvantaged child be taught?', *Child Development*, 40, 47–61.
Block, J. H. (ed.) (1971), *Mastery Learning—Theory and Practice*, New York, Holt.
Block, N. and Dworking, G. (eds) (1977), *The IQ Controversy*, London, Quartet Books.
Bloom, B. S. (1971), 'Mastery learning', in Block, J. H. (ed.), *Mastery Learning*, New York, Holt.
Bloom, B. S. (ed.) (1956), *Taxonomy of Educational Objectives: Handbook I, Cognitive Domains*, New York, David McKay Company.
Bolton, N. (1972), *The Psychology of Thinking*, London, Methuen.
Bortner, M. and Birch, H. G. (1970), 'Cognitive capacity and cognitive competence', *Americal Journal of Mental Deficiency*, 74, 735–44.
Bower, T. G. R. (1974), *Development in Infancy*, San Francisco, Freeman.
Bower, T. G. R. (1977), *A Primer of Infant Development*, San Francisco, W. H. Freeman and Company.
Brody, E. B. and Brody, N. (1976), *Intelligence—Nature, Determinants and Consequences*, New York, Academic Press.
Bronfenbrenner, U. (1975), 'Is early intervention effective?', in Bronfenbrenner and Mahoney (eds), (1975).
Bronfenbrenner, U. and Mahoney, M. A. (eds) (1975), *Influences on Human Development* (second edition), Hinsdale, Illinois, Dryden Press.
Brown, G. and Desforges, C. (1977), 'Piagetian psychology and education: time for revision', *British Journal of Educational Psychology*, 47, 7–17.
Bruner, J. S. (1960), *The Process of Education*, Cambridge, Mass., Harvard University Press.
Bruner, J. S. (1964), 'The course of cognitive growth', *American Psychologist*, 19, 1–15.
Bruner, J. S., Olver, R. R. and Greenfield, P. M. et al. (1966), *Studies in Cognitive Growth*, New York, Wiley.
Bruner, J. S., Jolly, A. and Sylva, K. (eds) (1976), *Play—Its Role in Development and Evolution*, Harmondsworth, Penguin.
Bryans, T. and Wolfendale, S. (1973), *Guidelines for Teachers*, no. 1, London Borough of Croydon.
Bryant, P. (1974), *Perception and Understanding in Young Children: An Experimental Approach*, London, Methuen.
Bullock Report (1975), *A Language for Life*, London, HMSO.
Burt, C. (1921), *Mental and Scholastic Tests*, London, King.
Burt, C. (1949), 'The Structure of the Mind', *British Journal of Educational Psychology*, 19, 110–11 and 176–99.
Burt, C. (1954), 'Differentiation of intellectual ability', *British Journal of Educational Psychology*, 24, 76–90.
Burt, C. (1966), 'The genetic determination of differences in intelligence: a study of monozygotic twins reared together and apart', *British Journal of Educational Psychology*, 57, 146.

Bibliography

Butcher, H. J. (1968), *Human intelligence—its nature and assessment*, London, Methuen.
Butcher, H. J. and Lomax, D. E. (eds) (1972), *Readings in Human Intelligence*, London, Methuen

Caldwell, B. M. (1967), 'What is the Optimal Learning Environment for the Young Child?' *American Journal of Orthopsychiatry*, 37.
Callaway, W. R. (1970), 'Modes of biological adaptation and their role in intellectual development', *PCD Monographs*, 1.
Cancro, R. (ed.) (1971), *Intelligence–Genetic and Environmental Influences*, New York, Grune & Stratton.
Cattell, R. B. (1971), *Abilities: Their Structure, Growth and Action*, Boston, Houghton Mifflin.
Chomsky, N. (1968), *Language and Mind*, New York, Harcourt, Brace.
Clarke, A. D. B. (1978), 'Predicting human development: Problems, evidence, implications', *Bulletin of the British Psychological Society*, 31, 249–58
Clarke, A. D. B. and Clarke, A. M. (1972), 'Consistency and variability in the growth of human characteristics', in Wall, W. D. and Varma, V. P. (eds), *Advances in Educational Psychology*, University of London Press, vol. 1, pp. 33–52.
Clarke, A. M. and Clarke, A. D. B. (eds) (1974), *Mental Deficiency—The Changing Outlook*, London, Methuen.
Clarke, A. M. and Clarke, A. D. B. (1976a), 'Problems in comparing the effects of environmental change at different ages', in McGurk (ed.), *Ecological Factors in Human Development*, Amsterdam, North Holland Publishing Company.
Clarke, A. M. and Clarke, A. D. B. (eds) (1976b), *Early Experience: Myth and Evidence*, London, Open Books.
Clarke, A. M. and Clarke, A. D. B. (1978), 'Early experience: its limited effects upon later development', in Shaffer, D. and Dunn, J. F. (eds), *The First Year of Life*, New York, Wiley.
Cole, M. and Bruner, J. S. (1971), 'Cultural differences and inferences about psychological processes', *American Psychologist*, 26, 867–76.
Cooper, J., Moodley, M. and Reynell, J. (1978), *Helping Language Development*, London, Edward Arnold.
Craik, F. I. M. and Lockhart, R. S. (1972), 'Levels of processing: a framework for memory research', *Journal of Verbal Learning and Verbal Behaviour*, 11, 671–84.

Davie, R., Butler, N. and Goldstein, H. (1972), *From Birth to Seven: A report of the National Child Development Study*, London, Longmans and the National Children's Bureau.
Davis, K. (1947), 'Final note on a case of extreme isolation', *American Journal of Sociology*, 45, 554–65.
Dobbing, J. and Smart, J. L. (1974), 'Vulnerability of developing brain and behaviour', *British Medical Bulletin*, 30, 164–8.
Dockrell, W. B. (ed.) (1970), *On Intelligence*, London, Methuen.
Donaldson, M. (1963), *A Study of Children's Thinking*, London, Tavistock.
Donaldson, M. (1978), *Children's Minds*, Glasgow, Collins.
Douglas, J. W. B. (1964), *The Home and the School*, London, MacGibbon & Kee.

Bibliography

Douglas, J. W. B., Ross, J. M. and Simpson, H. R. (1968), *All Our Future*, London, Peter Davies.
Dunn, L. M. (1968), 'Special education for the mildly retarded—is much of it justifiable?', *Exceptional Children*, 34, 5–22.

Ebbinghaus, H. (1897), 'Über eine neue Methode zur Prüfing geistiger Fähigkeiten und ihre Anwendung bei Schulkindern', *Zeitschrift für Angewandte Psychologie*, 92, 331–4.
Elkind, D. (1971), 'Two approaches to intelligence: Piagetian and psychometric', from Green, D. R., Ford, M. P. and Flamer, G. B., *Measurement and Piaget* (Proceedings of the CTB/McGraw-Hill Conference on Ordinal Scales of Cognitive Development). Reproduced in Sants. J. and Butcher H. J. (eds), *Developmental Psychology: Selected Readings* (1975), Harmondsworth, Pengiun.
Elliott, C. (1975), 'The British Intelligence Scale: final report before standardisation, 1975–76', papers presented at the Annual Conference of the British Psychological Society, 1975. Published in *Occasional Papers of the Division of Educational and Child Psychology of the B.P.S.*, Issue 10, Spring 1976.
Elliott, C. (1976), 'The measurement of development', In Varma, V. P. and Williams, P. (eds), *Piaget, Psychology and Education*, London, Hodder & Stoughton.
Elliott, C., Murray, D. J. and Pearson, L. S. (1978), *British Ability Scales—Manuals*, Windsor, NFER.
Erlenmeyer-Kimling, L. (1977), 'Gene—Environment Interactions and the Variability of Behaviour', in Ehrman, L., Omenn, G. S. and Caspari, E. (eds), *Genetics, Environment and Behaviour*, New York, Academic Press.
Erlenmeyer-Kimling, L. and Jarvik, L. F. (1963), 'Genetics and Intelligence', *Science*, 142, 1477–9.
Eysenck, H. J. (1967), 'Intelligence assessment: a theoretical and experimental approach', *British Journal of Educational Psychology*, 37, 81–98.
Eysenck, H. J. (1971), *Race, Intelligence and Education*, London, Temple Smith.
Eysenck, H. J. (ed.) (1973), *The Measurement of Intelligence*, Lancaster, Medical and Technical Press.

Farnham-Diggory, S. (1972), *Cognitive Processes in Education: A Psychological Preparation for Teaching and Curriculum Development*, New York, Harper & Row.
Ferguson, G. A. (1954), 'On learning and human ability', *Canadian Journal of Psychology*, 8, 95–112.
Feuerstein, R. (1971), 'Low functioning children in residential and day settings for the deprived', in Wollins, M. and Cottesman, M. (eds), *Group Care: an Israeli approach*, New York, Gordon & Breach.
Fogelman, K. R. and Goldstein, H. (1976), 'Social factors associated with changes in educational attainment between 7 and 11 years of age', *Educational Studies*, 2, 95–109.
Fontana, D. (ed.) (1978), *The Education of the Young Child*, London, Open Books.
Francis, H. (1977), *Language in Teaching and Learning*, London, George Allen & Unwin.
Fraser, E. D. (1959), *Home Environment and the School* (with a Postscript) (Postscript, 1973), University of London Press.

Bibliography 113

Gagné, R. M. (1974), *Essentials of Learning for Instruction*, Hinsdale, Illinois, Dryden Press.

Gagné, R. M. (1977), *The Conditions of Learning* (third edition), New York, Holt, Rinehart & Winston.

Gagné, R. M. and Briggs, L. J. (1974), *Principles of Instructional Design*, New York, Holt, Rinehart & Winston.

Galton, F. (1883), *Inquirie into human faculty and its development*, New York, Macmillan.

Garber, H. and Heber, F. R. (1977), 'The Milwaukee Project—indications of the effectiveness of early intervention in preventing mental retardation', in Mittler, P. (ed.), *Research to Practice in Mental Retardation*, vol. I: *Care and Intervention*, IASSMD, University Park Press, Baltimore.

Garrett, H. E.. (1946), 'A developmental theory of intelligence', *American Psychologist*, 1, 372–8.

Gillham, W. E. C. (1978), 'Measurement constructs and psychological structures: Psychometrics', in Burton, J. and Radford, A., *Thinking in perspective—critical essays in the study of thought processes*, London, Methuen.

Ginsburg. H. (1972), *The Myth of the Deprived Child: Poor Children's Intellect and Education*, Englewood Cliffs, New Jersey, Prentice-Hall.

Glaser, R. (1963), 'Institutional technology and the measurement of learning outcomes', *American Psychologist*, 18, 519–21.

Golby, M., Greenwald, J. and West, R. (eds) (1975), *Curriculum Design*, London, Croom Helm/Open Univeristy Press.

Gordon, H. (1923), *Mental and Scholastic Tests among Retarded Children*, London, Board of Education Pamphlet, no. 44.

Gray, S. W. and Klaus, R. A. (1965), 'An experimental pre-school programme for culturally deprived children', *Child Development*, 36, 887–98.

Gray, S. W. and Klaus, R. A. (1970), 'The Early Training Project: a seventh year report', *Child Development*, 41, 909–24.

Guilford, J. P. (1959), 'Three faces of intellect', *American Psychologist*, 14, 469–79.

Guilford, J. P. (1967), *The Nature of Human Intelligence*, New York, McGraw-Hill.

Guilford, J. P. and Hoepfner, R. (1971), *The Analysis of Intelligence*, New York, McGraw-Hill.

Hambleton, R. K., Swaminathan, H., Algina, J. and Coulson, D. B. (1978), 'Criterion-referenced testing and measurement: a review of technical issues and developments', *Review of Educational Research*, 48, 1–47.

Hamilton, D., Jenkins, D., King, C., Macdonald, B. and Parlett, M. (1977), *Beyond the Numbers Game*, London, Macmillan.

Hamilton, V. and Vernon, M. D. (eds) (1976), *The Development of Cognitive Processes*, London, Academic Press.

Hammill, D. D. and Larsen, S. C. (1974), 'The effectiveness of psycholinguistic training', *Exceptional Children*, September 1974.

Harlow, H. F. (1949), 'The formation of learning sets', *Psychological Review*, 56, 51–65

Hebb, D.O. (1949), *The Organisation of Behaviour*, New York, Wiley.

Hebb, D. O. (1966), *Textbook of Psychology*, Philadelphia, Saunders.

Heber, R. (1971), *Rehabilitation of Families at Risk for Mental Retardation: a*

Progress Report, Madison, Wisconsin: Rehabilitation Research and Training Centre in Mental Retardation.
Heber, R. and Garber, H. (1971), 'An experiment in prevention of cultural-familial mental retardation', *Proceedings of the Second Congregation of the International Association for the Scientific Study of Mental Deficiency*, D. A. Primrose (ed.), Warsaw, Polish Medical Publishers: Amsterdam, Swets & Zeitlinger, pp. 31–5.
Heim, A. W. (1975), *Psychological Testing*, Oxford University Press.
Hess, R. D. and Shipman, V. C. (1965), 'Early experience and the socialization of cognitive modes in children', *Child Development*, 36, 869–86.
Hindley, C. B. (1965), 'Stability and change in abilities up to five years: group trends', *Journal of Child Psychology and Psychiatry*, 6, 85–99.
Hofstaetter, P. R. (1954), 'The changing composition of "intelligence": a study in T-technique', *Journal of Genetic Psychology*, 85, 159–64.
Holt, J. (1964), *How Children Fail*, New York, Pitman.
Howe, M. J. A. (1972), *Understanding School Learning—a New Look at Educational Psychology*, New York, Harper & Row.
Howe, M. J. A. (1975), *Learning in Infants and Young Children*, London, Macmillan.
Howe, M. J. A. (1976), 'Good learners and poor learners', *Bulletin of the British Psychological Society*, 29, 16–19.
Humphreys, L. G. (1971), 'Theory of intelligence', in Cancro, R. (ed.), *Intelligence: Genetic and Environmental Influences*, New York, Grune & Stratton.
Hunt, J. McV. (1961), *Intelligence and Experience*, New York, Ronald Press Co.
Hunt, J. McV. (1971), 'Using intrinsic motivation to teach young children', *Educational Technology*, II, no. 2, 78–80.
Hunt, J. McV. and Kirk, G. E. (1974), 'Criterion-referenced tests of school readiness: a paradigm with illustrations', *Genetic Psychology Monographs*, 90, 114–82

Jarman, R. F. (1978), 'Level I and Level II abilities: Some theoretical reinterpretations', *British Journal of Psychology*, 69, 257–69.
Jensen, A. R. (1969), 'How much can we boost IQ and scholastic achievement?' *Harvard Educational Review*, 39, 1–123.
Jensen, A. R. (1970), 'Hierarchical theories of mental ability', in Dockrell, W. B. (ed.), *On Intelligence*, London, Methuen.
Jensen, A. R. (1973a), *Educability and Group Differences*, London, Methuen.
Jensen, A. R. (1973b), *Educational Differences*, London, Methuen.
Johnson, D. and Myklebust, H. (1967), 'Learning disabilities: educational principles and practice', New York, Grune & Stratton.

Kagan, J. (1966), 'Developmental studies in reflection and analysis', in Kidd, A. H. and Rivoire, J. E. (eds), *Perceptual Development in Children*, New York, International Universities Press.
Kagan, J. (1970), 'Attention and psychological change in the young child', *Science*, 170, 826–32.
Kagan, J. (1976), 'Resilience and continuity in psychological development', in Clarke, A. M. and Clarke, A. D. B. (eds), *Early Experience*, London, Open Books.

Kagan, J. and Lang, C. (1978), *Psychology and Education—An Introduction*, New York, Harcourt Brace Jovanovich.
Kamin, L. J. (1974), *The Science of Politics of I.Q.*, Potomac, Md., Lawrence Erlbaum Associates.
Karnes, M. B., Teska, J. A. and Hodgins, A. S. (1970), 'The effects of four programs of classroom intervention on the intellectual and language development of 4-year-old disadvantaged children', *American Journal of Orthopsychiatry*, 40, 58–76.
Kaufman, A. F. and Kaufman, N. L. (1977), *Clinical Evaluation of Young Children with the McCarthy Scales*, New York, Grune & Stratton.
Kiernan, C. and Jones, M. (1977), *Behaviour Assessment Battery*, Windsor, NFER.
Kirk, S. A. and Kirk, W. D. (1971), *Psycholinguistic Learning Disabilities: Diagnosis and Remediation*, Urbana, University of Illinois Press.
Kirk, S. A., McCarthy, J. J. and Kirk, W. D. (1968), *Examiner's Manual for the Illinois Test of Psycholinguistic Abilities*, second edition, Urbana, University of Illinois Press.
Klausmeier, H. J. (1976), 'Instructional design and the teaching of concepts', in Levin, J. R. and Allen, V. L. (eds), *Cognitive Learning in Children: Theories and Strategies*, New York, Academic Press.
Koluchova, J. (1972), 'Severe deprivation in twins: a case study', *Journal of Child Psychology and Psychiatry*, 13, 107–14 (reprinted in Clarke, A. M. and Clarke A. D. B. (eds), *Early Experience*, London, Open Books 1976).
Koluchova, J. (1976), 'A report on the further development of twins after severe and prolonged deprivations', in Clarke, A. M. and Clarke, A. D. B. (eds) *Early Experience: Myth and Evidence*, London, Open Books.

Labouvie-Vief, G. (1976), 'Intellectual abilities and learning: retrospect and prospect', in Levin, J. R. and Allen, V. L. (eds), *Cognitive Learning in Children: Theories and Strategies*, New York, Academic Press.
Labov, W. (1969), 'The logic of nonstandard English', *Georgetown Monographs on Language and Linguistics*, 22, 1–31, (excerpts reprinted in Giglioli, P. P. (ed.), *Language and Social Context*, Harmondsworth, Penguin).
Leach, D. J. and Raybould, E. C. (1977), *Learning and Behaviour Difficulties in School*, London, Open Books.
Lesser, G. S., Fifer, G. and Clarke, D. H. (1965), 'Mental abilities of children from different social-class and cultural groups', *Monographs of the Society for Research in Child Development*, 30, no. 4.
Lewin, R. (ed.) (1975), *Child Alive*, London, Temple-Smith.
Lewin, R. (1977), 'Head Start Pays Off', *New Scientist*, 3 March 1977.
Li, C. C. (1971), 'A tale of two thermos bottles: properties of a genetic model for human intelligence', in Cancro, R. (ed.), *Intelligence—Genetic and Environmental Influences*, New York, Grune & Stratton.
Lovell, K. (1968), 'The relationship between language and thought', in McComisky, J. G. (ed.), *Psychological Research and the Teacher, Aspects of Education—Seven*, Journal of the Institute of Education, Hull University.
Lunzer, E. A. (1970), *On Children's Thinking*, Windsor, NFER.
Lunzer, E. A. (1976), 'An appreciation of Piaget's work', in Varma, V. P. and Williams, P. (eds), *Piaget, Psychology and Education*, London, Hodder & Stoughton.

Luria, A. R. and Yudovich, F. I. (1959), *Speech and the Development of Mental Processes in the Child*, London, Staples Press.

McCall, R. B., Appelbaum, M. I. and Hogarty, P. S. (1973), 'Developmental changes in mental performance', *Monographs of the Society for Research in Child Development*, 38, no. 3.

McCarthy, M. (1970), *McCarthy Scales of Children's Abilities—Manual*, New York, The Psychological Corporation.

McFarland, H. S. N. (1971), *Psychological Theory and Educational Practice: Human Development, Learning and Assessment*, London, Routledge & Kegan Paul.

McNemar, Q. (1964), 'Lost: our intelligence? Why?', *American Psychologist*, 19, 871–82

Man: A Course of Study (1970), *Evaluation Strategies*. Based on research by D. White, J. P. Hanley, E. W. Moo and A. Walter in the Educational Development Centre, Washington, D.C., Curriculum Development Associates.

Mause, L. de (1974), 'The evolution of childhood', *History of Childhood Quarterly*, 1, no. 4.

Miles, T. R. (1957), 'Contributions to intelligence testing and the theory of intelligence. I. On defining intelligence', *British Journal of Educational Psychology*, 27, 153–65.

Miller, G. A., Galanter, E. and Pribram, K. H. (1960), *Plans and the Structure of Behaviour*, New York, Holt.

Mischel, W. (1968), *Personality and Assessment*, New York, Wiley.

Morris, J. M. (1966), *Standards and Progress in Reading*, Slough, NFER.

Mussen, P. H., Conger, J. J. and Kagan, J. (1974), *Child Development and Personality*, fourth edition, New York, Harper & Row.

Neisser, U. (1967), *Cognitive Psychology*, New York, Appleton-Century-Crofts.

Neisser, U. (1976), *Cognition and Reality: Principles and Implications of Cognitive Psychology*, San Francisco, W. H. Freeman.

Newcomer, P. and Hammill, D. D. (1975), 'The ITPA and academic achievement: a survey of the literature', *The Reading Teacher*, 28, 731—41.

Nisbet, J. D. and Entwistle, N. J. (1967), 'Intelligence and family size', 1949–65, *British Journal of Educational Psychology*, 37, 188–93.

Osgood, C. E. (1957), 'A behavioristic analysis of perception and language as cognitive phenomena', in *Contemporary Approaches to Cognition*, Cambridge, Mass., Harvard University Press.

Owen, L. and Stoneman, C. (1972), 'Education and the Nature of Intelligence', in Rubinstein, D. and Stoneman, C. (eds), *Education for Democracy* (second edition), Harmondsworth, Penguin.

Paraskevopoulos, J. M. and Kirk, S. A. (1969), *The Development and Psychometric Characteristics of the Revised Illinois Test of Psycholinguistic Abilities*, Urbana, University of Illinois Press.

Piaget, J. (1950), *The Psychology of Intelligence*, London, Routledge & Kegan Paul.

Piaget, J. (1967), *The Origins of Intelligence in Children*, New York, International University Press.

Pidgeon, D. A. (1970), *Expectation and Pupil Performance*, Windsor NFER.
Pilling, D. and Pringle, M. K. (1978), *Controversial Issues in Child Development*, London, Elek.

Rapier, J. L. (1962), 'Measured intelligence and the ability to learn', *Acta Pyschologica*, 1962, 1–17.
Resnick, L. B. (ed.) (1976), *The Nature of Intelligence*, Hillsdale, New Jersey, Lawrence Erlbaum Associates.
Riding, R. J. (1977), *School Learning: Mechanisms and Processes*, London, Open Book.
Rose, S. (1972), 'Environmental Effects on Brain and Behaviour', in Richardson, K. and Spears, D. (eds), *Race, Culture and Intelligence*, Harmondsworth, Penguin.
Rosenthal, D. (1968), 'The genetics of intelligence and personality', in Glass, D. C. (ed.), *Biology and Behavior—Genetics*, New York, Rockefeller University Press and Russell Sage Foundation.
Rosenthal, R. and Jacobson, L. (1968), *Pygmalion in the Classroom*, New York, Holt, Rinehart & Winston.
Ross, A. D. (1976), *Psychological Aspects of Learning Disabilities and Reading Disorders*, New York, McGraw-Hill.
Rutter, M. (1975), *Helping Troubled Children*, Harmondsworth, Penguin.
Rutter, M. and Madge, N. (1976), *Cycles of Disadvantage: A Review of Research*, London, Heinemann.
Ryan, J. (1972), 'IQ—the illusion of objectivity', in Richardson, K. and Spears, D. (eds), *Race, Culture and Intelligence*, Harmondsworth, Penguin.
Ryle, G. (1949), *The Concept of Mind*, London, Hutchinson.

Sameroff, A. J. and Chandler, M. J. (1975), 'Reproductive risk and the continuum of caretaking casualty', in Horowitz, F. D., Hetherington, E. M., Scarr-Salapatek, S. and Siegel, G. M. (eds), *Review of Child Development Research*, vol, 4, Uniersity of Chicago Press.
Sattler, J. M. (1974), *Assessment of Children's Intelligence*, Philadelphia, W. B. Saunders.
Schmidt, W. H. O. (1973), *Child Development: The Human, Cultural and Educarional Context*, New York, Harper & Row.
Searls, E. F. (1975), *How to Use WISC Scores in Reading Diagnosis*, Newark, Delaware, IRA.
Serpell, R. (1976), *Culture's Influence on Behaviour*, London, Methuen.
Sherman, M. and Key, C. B. (1932), 'The intelligence of isolated mountain children', *Child Development*, 3, 279–90.
Simon, B. (1971), *Intelligence, Psychology and Education*, London, Lawrence and Wishart.
Skeels, H. M. and Dye, H. B. (1939), 'A study of the effects of differential stimulation on mentally retarded children', *Proceedings of the American Association of Mental Deficiency*, 44, 114–36.
Skemp, R. R. (1962), 'The need for a schematic learning theory', *British Journal of Educational Psychology*, 32, 133–42.
Skemp, R. R. (1971), *The Psychology of Learning Mathematics*, Harmondsworth, Penguin.

Bibliography

Skodak, M. and Skeels, H. M. (1949), 'A final follow-up study of one hundred adopted children', *Journal of Genetic Psychology*, 75, 85–125.

Smedslund, J. (1977), 'Piaget's Psychology in Practice', *British Journal of Educational Psychology*, 47, 1–6.

Spearman, C. (1904), '"General Intelligence" objectively determined and measured', *American Journal of Psychology*, 15, 201–92.

Staats, A. W. (1971), *Child learning, intelligence, and personality*, Ne York, Harper & Row.

Staats, A. W. (1971), *Child Learning, Intelligence, and Personality*, New York, development: representative samples, cumulative-hierarchical learning, and experimental-longitudinal methods', *Monographs of the Society for Research in Child Development*, 35, no. 8.

Stenhouse, L. (1975), *An Introduction to Curriculum Research and Development*, London, Heinemann.

Stevens, M. (1976), *The Educational and Social Needs of Children with Severe Handicap* (second edition), London, Edward Arnold.

Stinchcombe, A. L. (1969), 'Environment: the cumulation of effects is yet to be understood', *Harvard Educational Review*, 39, 511–22.

Stones, E. (1969), 'The evaluation of learning', *British Journal of Medical Education*, 3, 135–42 (abridged version reprinted in Stones, E. (ed.), *Readings in Educational Psychology* (1970), Methuen, London).

Stott, D. H. (1978a), 'Harnessing children's play to the business of learning', *Oxford Educational Review*, 4, 65–76.

Stott, D. H. (1978b), *Helping Children with Learning Difficulties*, London, Ward Lock.

Swift, D. F. (1968), 'Social class and achievement motivation', *Educational Research*, 8, 83–95.

Thorndike, R. L. (1963), *The Concepts of Over and Under-achievement*, New York, Columbia.

Thurstone, L. L. (1938), 'Primary Mental Abilities', *Psychometric Monograph*, no. 4.

Thurstone, L. L. (1948), 'Psychological implications of factor analysis', *American Psychologist*, 3, 402–8.

Tough, J. (1976), *Listening to Children Talking—a Guide to the Appraisal of Children's Use of Language*, London, Ward Lock/Schools Council.

Turner, J. (1977), *Psychology for the Classroom*, London, Methuen.

Uzgiris, I. C. (1970), 'Sociocultural factors in cognitive development', in Haywood, H. C. (ed.), *Social-Cultural Aspects of Mental Retardation*, New York, Appleton-Century-Crofts.

Uzgiris, I. C. and Hunt, J. McV. (1975), *Assessment in Infancy: Ordinal Scales of Psychological Development*, Urbana, University of Illinois Press.

Varma, V. P. and Williams, P. (eds) (1976), *Piaget, Psychology and Education*, London, Hodder & Stoughton.

Vernon, P. E. (1950), *The Structure of Human Abilities*, London, Methuen.

Vernon, P. E. (1960), *Intelligence and Attainment Tests*, University of London Press.

Bibliography

Vernon, P. E. (1968), 'What is potential ability', *Bulletin of the British Psychological Society*, 21, 211–19.
Vernon, P. E. (1969), *Intelligence and Cultural Environment*, London, Methuen.
Vernon, P. E. (1970), 'Intelligence', in Dockrell, W. B. (ed.), *On Intelligence*, London, Methuen.
Vernon, P. E. (1971), 'Analysis of cognitive ability', *British Medical Bulletin*, 27, 222–6.
Vernon, P. E. (1976a), 'Environment and intelligence', in Varma, V. P. and Williams, P. (eds), *Piaget. Psychology and Education*, London, Hodder & Stoughton.
Vernon, P. E. (1976b), 'Development of intelligence', in Hamilton, V. and Vernon, M. D. (eds), *The Development of Cognitive Processes*, London, Academic Press.
Vygotsky, L. S. (1962), *Thought and Language*, Cambridge, Mass., MIT Press.

Ward, J. (1970), 'On the concept of criterion-referenced measurement', *British Journal of Educational Psychology*, 40, 314–23.
Warnock Report (1978), *Special Educational Needs*, London, HMSO.
Wechsler, D. (1966), 'The I.Q. is an intelligent test', *New York Times*, 26 June (reprinted in Edwards, A. J. (ed.), *Selected Papers of David Wechsler* (1974), New York, Academic Press).
Wechsler, D. (1974), *WISC-R Manual*, NFER, Windsor (anglicized version).
Wedell, K. (1973), *Learning and Perceptuo-motor Disabilities in Children*, London, Wiley.
Wedge, P. and Prosser, H. (1973), *Born to Fail?* London, National Children's Bureau/Arrow Books.
Wheeler, L. R. (1942), 'A comparative study of the intelligence of East Tennessee mountain children', *Journal of Educational Psychology*, 33, 321–4.
Williams, M. (1976), *Personality and Learning*, Block 7, Part 2, Milton Keynes, Open University.
Wiseman, S. (1964), *Education and Environment*, Manchester University Press.
Witkin, H. A., Dyk, R. B., Faterson, H. F., Goodenough, D. R. and Karp, S. A. (1962), *Psychological Differentiation: Studies of Mental Development*, New York, Wiley
Wolf, T. H. (1973), *Alfred Binet*, University of Chicago Press.
Woodward, W. M. (1971). *The Development of Behaviour*, Harmondsworth, Penguin.

Yule, W., Rutter, M., Berger, M. and Thompson, J. (1974), 'Over- and under-achievement in reading: distribution in the general population', *British Journal of Educational Psychology*, 44, 1–12.

Zajonc, R. (1975), 'IQ—The first shall be first', *Psychology Today* (UK edition, May 1975).

Index

ability, *see* intelligence
accommodation, 80
actions, *see* thinking—sensori-motor
adaptation, 3, 14–15, 80
assimilation, 80
attempts to raise IQ, 61 f, 99

behaviourist approaches, 68, 93 f
Binet, A., 3, 16, 22 f, 27 f, 32, 75
biological factors, 48 f, 54 f, 64 f, 67
brain development, 54
British Ability Scales (BAS), 40 f, 47, 86
Bruner, J. S., 70, 72, 74, 78 f, 96, 101
Burt, C., 3, 8, 10, 24, 53

capacity, 2, 18, 87 f
Clarke, A. D. B., 66, 70
Clarke, A. D. B. and Clarke, A. M., 18, 54, 56, 64, 65, 66, 76
cognitive conflict, 14–15, 79–80, 104
cognitive development, 68 f; *see also* thinking
cognitive factors, 60 f
cognitive skills, *see* skills
compensatory education, 40, 52, 61 f, 65, 88
concepts, 70 f, 82; *see also* thinking
conservation, 76
constancy of IQ, 65
correlation coefficient, 7
criterion-referenced tests, 36 f, 47, 97, 98, 100
criticisms of IQ testing, 33 f, 98; *see also* criterion-referenced tests

crystallised intelligence (g_c), 13
cultural factors, 55 f, 72; *see also* environmental factors

description *v.* explanation, 55, 69, 93 f
developmental approaches to intelligence, 14 f, 68 f, 72 f, 93 f
differentiation of abilities, 9, 17
disadvantaged children, 6, 13, 17, 39, 75 f; *see also* compensatory education

early experience, 65
educationally subnormal children (ESN), *see* mental handicap
enactive mode, 74, 78
environmental factors, 6, 15, 48 f, 55 f, 64 f, 66 f, 79–80
equilibration, 80
experimental measures of intelligence, 37 f, 93 f

factor analysis, 9
factors associated with intelligence, *see* biological factors *and* environmental factors
family and home background, 57 f, 66
feedback, 95 f
'fixed' intelligence, 18, 19, 49 f
fluid intelligence (g_f), 13

gene-environment interaction, *see* interactions
general intelligence ('g'), 7 f, 17, 20, 23, 47

121

Index

genetics, 49, 50 f, 66
genotype, 15, 20
group factors, 9
Guilford, J. P., 4, 10, 11, 17, 69, 82, 93, 98

Headstart, *see* compensatory education
Hebb, D. O., 15, 17, 20, 64, 88
heredity/hereditary factors, *see* genetics
heritability coefficient, 48 f, 53
hierarchical models, 8 f
Hunt, J. McV., 17, 37, 38, 59, 80, 86, 100 f
hypothetical construct, 2, 18, 19, 21, 34, 104

iconic mode, 7, 48, 78
Illinois Test of Psycholinguistic Ability (ITPA), 44 f, 86, 98
images, 70, 82
impulsivity-reflectivity, 82
'innate' ability, 5, 19; *see also* interactions *and* biological factors
intellectual ability and learning, 92 f
intellectual development, 68 f; *see also* thinking
intellectual skills, *see* skills
intelligence: A and B, 15 f, 47, 48, 88; definitions of, 1 f; and latent traits, *see* hypothetical constructs; models of, 6 f; reification of, 5; and school achievement/attainment, 4, 17, 89 f; and stages of development, 2, 72 f; and underlying processes, *see* hypothetical constructs; and teaching, 36 f, 40, 44, 58, 60–1, 77, 85 f, 89 f, 93 f, 98 f
intelligence quotient (IQ), 2, 18, 20 f, 34, 52 f, 67, 89 f; consistency and variability of, 65 f; deviation IQs, 32
intelligence tests, 17, 20 f; criterion-referenced, 36 f, 47, 97, 98, 100; criticisms of, 33 f, 98; group, 26 f; historical background, 21 f; individual, 26 f; non-verbal, 26–7; norm-referenced, 24 f, 36; profiles of, 31, 36, 41, 46; verbal, 26–7
intelligent behaviour, 5
interactions, 15, 64 f

Jensen, A. R., 13 f, 49, 52, 64

language: assessment, 39, 44 f; and cognitive development, 17, 60 f, 74, 77 f, 83 f; curriculum packages and kits, 46, 103
learning, 4, 17, 18, 19, 48, 93 f; events in, 94 f; transfer of, 16, 61, 95 f, 101 f; *see also* mini learning experiment
levels I and II ability, 17, 52
linguistic aspects, *see* language
longitudinal studies, 58, 62

mastery learning, 98
maturation, 50 f; *see also* biological factors *and* genetics
measurement of intelligence, *see* intelligence tests
memory, 81 f, 95 f
mental age (MA), 22 f, 27 f, 37, 68
mentally handicapped children, 17, 18, 37, 70
mental speed, 14, 41
Milwaukee project, 63
mini learning experiment, 18, 40, 101 f
modes of thinking, 73 f, 83, 99
multifaceted models of intelligence, 10 f, 19; *see also* Guilford, J. P. *and* skills

nature *v.* nurture, *see* innate ability; biological factors *and* environmental factors
non-verbal tests, 24 f, 33
normal distribution curve, 25, 98
norm-referenced tests, 24 f, 36

operations and operational thinking, 74 f
optimal learning environments, 94, 99 f
over-achievement, 90

perception and perceptual development, 73 f, 81 f, 95 f
performance, 2, 87 f
phases of learning, *see* events in learning
phenotype, 15, 20
Piaget, J., 3, 9, 14 f, 17, 37, 41, 70, 72, 74 f, 80, 83, 86

Index

practical intelligence and performance scales, 30 f
prediction of cognitive status, 14, 65, 70, 89 f
pre-operational thinking, 74 f
Primary Mental Abilities (PMAs), 10
'problem of the match', 59, 80, 100 f; *see also* Hunt, J. McV.
problem solving, 4, 97
processes of thinking, 80 f
psychometric models of intelligence, 6 f, 13 f, 17, 34, 68
psychosocial factors, *see* environmental factors

race studies, 51 f
Rasch scaling, 41
readiness, 17, 38 f, *see also* optimal learning environments
reflectivity-impulsivity, 82
regression equation, 91
reliability of tests, 26, 33, 46

schemas, 37, 70, 82
schooling, 59 f
self-fulfilling prophesy, 60
sensori-motor thinking, 37, 73 f
severely subnormal children, *see* mentally handicapped children
skills (cognitive and intellectual), 6, 16 f, 18, 20, 36 f, 44 f, 47, 48, 66 f, 72 f, 83 f, 95 f, 100
social class, 55 f, 66
spatial ability, 9; *see also* practical intelligence
Spearman, C., 3, 7, 23
specific abilities, 7, 20

stages of development, 74, 79, 83
standard deviation, 25 f
standard error, 25 f
standardised tests, *see* intelligence tests *and* norm-referenced tests
standard scores, 25 f, 33
Stanford-Binet intelligence scale, 27 f, 32
structure in learning, 87, 99 f
structure of intellect model, 11
symbolic mode of thinking, 74 f
symbols, 70

test-based models of intelligence, *see* psychometric models
thinking, 4, 73 f; generation and testing of hypotheses, 82; operational, 75 f; pre-operational, 75 f; processes of, 80 f, 93 f; sensori-motor, 73 f; units of, 70 f; what pushes thinking forward? 14–15, 79–80; *see also* language
transactions in development, 65, 100
twin studies, 53
two-factor model of intelligence, 7

underachievement, 87 f, 104
unitary models of intelligence, 19; *see also* general intelligence
units of intellectual development, 69, 70 f

validity of tests, 26, 32, 34, 47
verbal abilities and tests, 9, 24 f, 29 f
Vernon, P. E., 3, 4, 8, 15, 17, 57, 58, 61, 66, 90, 91

Wechsler, D., 3, 29 f
Wechsler tests of intelligence, 29 f, 36, 41